CW00739623

Helion & Company Limited
Unit 8 Amherst Business Centre
Budbrooke Road
Warwick
CV34 5WE
England
Tel. 01926 499 619
Email: info@helion.co.uk
Website: www.helion.co.uk
Twitter: @helionbooks
Visit our blog http://blog.helion.co.uk/

Text © Kevin Wright 2021
Photographs © as individually credited
Colour artworks © Tom Cooper 2021
Maps drawn by George Anderson and
    Tom Cooper, © Helion & Company/Tom
    Cooper respectively 2021

Designed and typeset by Farr out
    Publications, Wokingham, Berkshire
Cover design Paul Hewitt, Battlefield Design
    (www.battlefield-design.co.uk)

Every reasonable effort has been made to
trace copyright holders and to obtain their
permission for the use of copyright material.
The author and publisher apologise for any
errors or omissions in this work, and would
be grateful if notified of any corrections that
should be incorporated in future reprints or
editions of this book.

ISBN 978-1-914377-12-9

British Library Cataloguing-in-Publication
    Data
A catalogue record for this book is available
    from the British Library

We always welcome receiving book
proposals from prospective authors.

CONTENTS

Note: In order to simplify the use of this book, all names, locations and geographic
designations are as provided in *The Times World Atlas*, or other traditionally accepted major
sources of reference, as of the time of described events.

ABBREVIATIONS

AB	Air Base
ACAS (I)	Assistant Chief of the Air Staff (Intelligence) (RAF)
AFB	Air Force Base
AFSPPF	Air Force Special Projects Production Facility
ARC	Ad-hoc Requirements Committee
Art	Article, identification number given to CIA U-2s
ASARS	Advanced Synthetic Aperture Radar System
COMINT	Communications Intelligence
COMIREX	Committee on Imagery Requirements and Exploitation
COMOR	Committee on Overhead Reconnaissance
DCI	Director of Central Intelligence (CIA)
DPRK	Democratic People's Republic of Korea
ECCM	Electronic Counter Countermeasures
ECM	Electronic Countermeasures
EK	Eastman Kodak
ELINT	Electronic Intelligence
FAS	Federation of American Scientists
GCI	Ground Control Intercept
HMG	Her Majesty's Government
HTA	HT Automat
ICBM	Inter Continental Ballistic Missile
INS	Inertial Navigation System
IPIR	Initial Photographic Interpretation Report
IRBM	Intermediate-Range Ballistic Missile
JCS	Joint Chiefs of Staff
JIC	Joint Intelligence Committee (UK)
LOROP	Long Range Oblique Photography
MCP	Mission Coverage Plot
MoD	Ministry of Defence (UK)
NACA	National Advisory Committee for Aeronautics
NARA	National Archives and Records Administration
NAS	Naval Air Station
nm	nautical miles
NPIC	National Photographic Intelligence Center
NRO	National Reconnaissance Office

NSA	National Security Agency
NSC	National Security Council
OBC	Optical Bar Camera
ORBAT	Order of Battle
OSA	Office of Special Activities (CIA)
PI	Photographic Interpreter
PID	Photographic Interpretation Division
PoE	Point of Entry/Exit
RAE	Royal Aircraft Establishment
RTS	Reconnaissance Technical Squadron
SAC	Strategic Air Command
SACEUR	Supreme Allied Commander Europe
SAM	Surface to Air Missile
SIGINT	Signals intelligence (collective term for all forms of electronic signal collection)
SIS	Secret Intelligence Service
SYERS	SENIOR YEAR Electro-Optical Reconnaissance System
TDY	Tour of Duty
TELINT	Telemetry intelligence
TNA	The National Archive (UK)
UR-PIC	Temporary processing facilities deployed from Wiesbaden or Yakota
USAFE	US Air Forces Europe
USAFSS	US Air Force Security Service
USIB	US Intelligence Board
WRSP	Weather Reconnaissance Squadron (Provisional)

Cryptonyms

AQUATONE	CIA U-2 programme up to April 1958
CHALICE	CIA U-2 programme from April 1958
HBJAYWALK	Network for passing U-2 communications
IDEALIST	CIA U-2 programme from May 1960
JACKSON	UK participation in CIA U-2 Programme from October 1960
OLDSTER	UK participation in CIA U-2 Programme from June 1958

INTRODUCTION AND ACKNOWLEDGEMENTS

Developed in the mid-1950s the U-2 was and remains an astounding aircraft. Indeed, virtually everything about the whole U-2 project is remarkable. Some of the technical aspects are well known – its ability to fly at immense altitudes and its stunning photographic capabilities. Overshadowing its achievements was the very public loss of Gary Powers near Sverdlovsk on 1 May 1960.

Not only was its design and development a superlative achievement, in the field, the Central Intelligence Agency's original small fleet of 20 U-2As (supplemented by USAF airframes) operated across the world. The use of advanced technologies meant airframes were constantly being modified and updated. Operations were conducted in great secrecy and went to great trouble to hide their presence and role. Usually flying from remote locations, the aircraft,

without markings, often took-off before first light. Ostensibly operated by civilians, flying meteorological research missions their bold overflights took them far across Eastern Europe, the USSR and Far East. However, many details of the aircraft's operational history remain comparatively vague, and a considerable amount of detail still partially classified. Continuing national political sensitivities have meant that much about these early operations has never been fully revealed even more than 50 years later.

Whilst the U-2 was an enormous success the programme had its trials and tribulations. At the cutting edge of aerodynamics, aircraft engine design, electronics and optical technology it was hardly surprising there were hiccups. Issues of stability, engine reliability, growing payload weights, unreliable electronics and poor camera functioning all had to be overcome on occasion. That most of these difficulties were successfully resolved pays tribute to the skills and fortitude of Lockheed and other contractors and engineers involved, often working at austere forward bases. The U-2's use was of considerable political and military significance. For some years it was the most intrusive and successful intelligence gathering platform of all time.

This extensive account of the U-2's activities with the CIA is divided across two volumes. This one briefly covers early U-2 design and development but concentrates on overflights of Eastern Europe, the USSR and Middle East, up to when Gary Powers was shot down on Mayday 1960. To that are added details of RAF U-2 operations, missions conducted from Norway and Pakistan. It relies on declassified CIA records, many still significantly redacted, providing details of individual missions and operations. I also describe how the material collected by U-2 missions was processed and the intelligence used, by examining a few specific examples. From all this, I hope to present you with a slightly different perspective of

the history and achievements of the U-2. The second volume concentrates on Asian and worldwide operations across the rest of the world up to 1974.

This volume is the result of many hours working through CIA records, both a frustrating and rewarding experience. It has certainly been enlightening to plough through so much material about this fascinating aircraft and the extremely high value attached to the intelligence it collected. My thanks go to retired USAF U-2 pilots Lieutenant Colonels Bruce Jinneman and Rick Bishop for helping me understand the workings of the early U-2s and for sharing their experiences flying the aircraft. My thanks also to Eric Allen, Paul Lashmar, Chris Pocock, Paul Howard, Mick West, Akira Watanabe, Robert Hopkins, Ralf Manteufel, Kevin Slade, the Center for Strategic and International Studies and Center for the Study of National Reconnaissance for kindly allowing me to use their images. My special thanks to Dr Jason Ur for his help with imagery and maps and for allowing me to borrow widely from his research.

1

STOP GAP PLATFORM

The development of the U-2 from inception to the drawing board to first flight and operational missions was a remarkable achievement in a very short time. Much of this has been widely written about by others so is covered here only relatively briefly. Most of this chapter is devoted to an examination of the U-2's early sensor and equipment fits. These were so rapidly developed that individual airframes, in Lockheed and CIA phraseology referred to as 'Articles,' were often unique in their configuration at any one time.

The need for a reconnaissance aircraft that could outclass enemy defences had become obvious by the start of the Korean War. US losses from a few overflights and some coastal probing missions illustrated the shortcomings of existing designs. These were mainly based on modified Second World War aircraft or adaptions of early jet-engine designs. Just how unsatisfactory they were for gathering the large amounts of intelligence required from deeply intrusive overflights soon became very clear.

Intelligence Priorities

In the early 1950s US and British intelligence agencies desperately sought information on all Soviet nuclear activities. These included: research, manufacturing, testing, weapon storage, deployment and the bombers and missiles that carried them. The British priority was Soviet bombers and their bases as these posed the most immediate threat to the United Kingdom. The Americans believed Soviet missiles would soon pose an existential threat to the continental United States in a way the bombers likely would not. Their primary interest quickly focussed on Soviet missile development and deployment.

Strategic Air Command and RAF Bomber Command urgently needed detailed target intelligence on the Soviet bases from where nuclear attacks would be launched. Collecting that intelligence was largely dependent on making highly provocative overflights to photograph them. There was already a significant programme of US shallow penetration flights, largely against undefended or unsuspecting targets around the periphery of the USSR. These were

inadequate. Deep reconnaissance flights were needed. The early joint US and British experiences with deeper penetration overflights of the USSR, from 1953–56, under cover of darkness, whilst largely successful remained inadequate.

Operation Jiu Jitsu

In 1951 the Americans and British agreed that the RAF would undertake radar reconnaissance missions over targets, largely associated with Soviet nuclear bomber forces in the Western USSR. They used borrowed American RB-45C Tornado aircraft, British markings applied and flown by RAF crews. Squadron Leader John Crampton was appointed commander of the anodyne sounding 'Special Duties Flight' (SDF), flying from RAF Sculthorpe, a USAF RB-45C base in Norfolk. In late February 1952, Crampton was informed their mission was to acquire 'radarscope photography' of Soviet airbases and other important targets.

On 17 April, three RB-45Cs, left Sculthorpe. Air refuelled by USAF KB-29 tankers over Denmark and Germany flying at 36,000ft, they separated and flew three different routes. The northerly aircraft covered targets in the Baltic republics, the central route went well beyond Minsk in Belarus towards Moscow. The southerly route went past Kyiv and close to Rostov-on-Don in Ukraine. The distance the three aircraft penetrated Soviet controlled airspace is astounding, especially in the relatively slow RB-45s, albeit under cover of darkness. Crampton's own aircraft covered the greatest distance along the southern track and the mission lasted over 10 hours. All went relatively smoothly.

Called together for a second mission on 28–29 April 1954, they followed a similar plan. Each aircraft was again allocated a different route. Crampton headed towards Kyiv but Soviet air defences were far more active this time. He came under accurate, probably radar predicted, anti-aircraft fire that detonated at their 36,000ft altitude. Crampton pushed the aircraft to maximum speed and descended for some distance in an attempt to make life more difficult for the Soviet gunners. Following an abortive aerial refuelling as he returned over

Germany, he briefly diverted to Fürstenfeldbruck, their designated emergency diversion, then returned to Sculthorpe.[1]

Whilst Crampton and his colleagues showed great courage, indeed they were discreetly decorated, these flights exposed them to significant danger. However, their 'take' and that from other US penetration flights represented only a tiny proportion of the intelligence required. It was far from the systematic coverage necessary to provide comprehensive intelligence on Soviet bomber fields and high priority targets. The significance of the Jiu Jitsu flights was that they clearly illustrated how extensive a photo-reconnaissance effort would be needed to assemble a reliable, sufficiently detailed photographic intelligence picture. The existing means were inadequate, dangerous for the crews and risked political catastrophe. A much more radical approach was required.

Blueprint for the future

Well aware of the huge gaps in its knowledge of the Soviet Union, the US was determined to dramatically improve its intelligence collection capabilities. The 15 June 1952 Beacon Hill Report on 'Problems of Air Force Intelligence and Reconnaissance,' was compiled via the Massachusetts Institute of Technology.[2] It was a wide appraisal of technical collection methodologies and proposed an ambitious development agenda. It identified far-reaching measures to develop specialised aircraft and ultimately spaced based reconnaissance systems. Mainly overseen by a small group of scientists, it included chapters on photographic reconnaissance by James Baker and Edwin Land, developer of the 'Polaroid' instant camera. Beacon Hill identified the problems to be overcome to create useable imagery and makes informative reading even today. More immediately it laid out, to those privileged few allowed to see it, the enormous research effort required.

The main requirement was to develop comprehensive overhead coverage of the Soviet hinterland. A remarkable confluence of political will, scientific expertise and managerial determination developed what became the U-2, as a stopgap solution, until space-based systems became viable. That the U-2 flew as soon as it did, achieved deployment and performed amazing feats have turned its 'temporary' success into one that has lasted over 65 years.

Politics and Science

During the Second World War, Supreme Allied Commander of the Allied Expeditionary Force, General Dwight Eisenhower had regularly used photographic intelligence. He appreciated its value and shortcomings for politico-military decision-making. On entering the White House in January 1953, he brought that knowledge with him. He was determined to maintain pressure on the Soviet Union and publicly pursued initiatives to constrain their nuclear weapon development. Far from the public glare, in great secrecy, he oversaw the stepping up of penetration flights and the ill-fated reconnaissance balloon programmes against the USSR and China. More crucially, he harnessed the knowledge, experience and imagination of key individuals in the military, government, scientific and industrial communities and constructed the foundations for US reconnaissance policy and collection technology.

In the Beacon Hill report there is a brief mention of a reconnaissance aircraft promising superlative performance. In August 1954 James Killian's forward-looking Technological Capabilities Panel came behind the Lockheed 'CL-282.' This was Kelly Johnson's concept for a very high-flying aircraft, already rejected by the US Air Force.[3] Even with pressure from Eisenhower, CIA Director Alan Dulles was not keen to take on the project, until the President pushed responsibility for it onto the Agency.[4]

On 24 November 1954, Dulles committed Agency funds for the CL-282 to 'fill US overhead reconnaissance requirements.'[5] CIA responsibility for the design enabled a more secret, much less bureaucratically constrained effort and removed internal DoD politics than handing it to the Air Force would have done. On 26 November 1954, Richard Bissell, Special Assistant to Dulles, was assigned responsibility for the project. The use of CIA funds was easier to hide within the growing Agency budget in areas of expenditure largely unscrutinised by Congress. Removing it from the USAF budget had eased potential friction with them, as the Air Force hoped to gain an asset they had not paid for. Working with Air Force representatives, decisions were made to divert deliveries of the precious new J-57 engine to 'CL-282' production. The contract with Lockheed provided for 20 airframes to be supplied to the CIA at a total cost just under $19M with the first to be delivered in July 1955, initially working under the project name 'AQUATONE,' later 'CHALICE.'[6] It was accompanied by a USAF order for more than 30 U-2 airframes, contracted via the CIA.

Art 341, the first U-2. It was used as a test aircraft for its entire career, most notably for the 'Dirty Bird' project, until lost in 1957. (Lockheed Martin)

Johnson's Genius

The U-2 was a sensor-carrying platform, in essence, a powered glider, that took aeronautical design and construction to the limit of the day. It became a reality remarkably quickly and very cheaply by contemporary measures. That its same basic design is still in use today, over eight decades later, demonstrates just how remarkable it remains.

The U-2 was designed and constructed in great secrecy at Lockheed's Burbank 'Skunk Works' facility in California. Flown from Burbank in C-124s, early flight testing, development and training took place deep in the remote Nevada desert, at the Watertown strip, a facility owned by the US Atomic Energy Commission. Just eight months after the go-ahead on 26 November 1954, the first example (Art 341) flew, unintentionally becoming airborne there during a fast-taxi trial, on 27 July 1955. The U-2's wings developed high lift and it wanted to be airborne immediately. Pilots sometimes found it difficult to get out of the sky when trying to land.[7] Lockheed chief test pilot, Tony LeVier, led the rapidly expanding test programme until early September. An engine flameout problem soon emerged with the early J-57-P-37 interim engines. LeVier trained other Lockheed test pilots to fly the U-2, cascaded their skills to the CIA's carefully recruited 'civilian' and selected USAF pilots.

Watertown soon became a busy place. New aircraft would be delivered by C-124 and assembled in the small hangars at the site. They would be checked and flight tested. At the same time, pilots were being trained and becoming experienced on the new type. Technicians were soon discovering the U-2's technical foibles. Airframe modifications and newly developed photographic and ELINT equipment had to be incorporated as the whole operation moved forward. Preparations also began for deploying the aircraft operationally. Besides aircraft handling the pilots had to become proficient at long-range flights and maintaining accurate navigation mainly relying on the drift sight and the sextant where necessary. An updated version of the U-2's engine, the J57-P-31 arrived, less susceptible to flameouts than the original J57. It produced higher thrust and was lighter than the original '37' engine variant. Bringing

together all these aspects of the programme. Effectively testing and evaluating a new aircraft type straight off the production line, whilst simultaneously trying to ready it for urgent, seriously risky, operational tasks was a major task and soon achievement.

The U-2 operated at far higher altitudes than any other aircraft of its time, flying within the few knots of airspeed often described as the 'coffin corner.' The U-2's *never to exceed* velocity was Mach 0.8. At such altitudes, the gap between its never to exceed and stall speeds could be as low as six knots. On take-off it had to climb at very steep angles to avoid exceeding the Mach 0.8 upper limit, risking airframe damage. Once at operational heights, as the fuel burned off, altitude increased further and brought even greater safety from interception, although airspeed decreased even further. At 50,000ft speed was 160kts. At 62,000ft 130kts and at 72,000ft 104kts. Dependent on load and altitude, for the later U-2C, flying much slower than 80–100kts was close to stall speed.[8] At its astonishing operational altitudes, pilots wore a total pressure suit, designed by the David

U-2 'Articles' were airlifted into the Watertown site by C-124 and removed the same way for return to The *Skunk Works*. (Lockheed Martin)

At Watertown new airframes were assembled and maintained in the small hangars hastily constructed at the site. (Lockheed Martin)

As the U-2s approached entry into service they were marked in spurious NACA markings to substantiate their false identities as 'research' aircraft. (Lockheed Martin)

became apparent that fitted with the right equipment, U-2s could also detect and record electronic emissions and radio transmissions over considerable distances. That potentially offered an insight into Soviet radar, missile and communications technology.

Tracker Camera

It is useful to explain in a little more detail the 'form' and footprint that imagery took when it was brought to the Photo Interpreters. Tracking camera images covered a very wide swath of territory. Each frame was sequentially numbered with a clock time printed on it. This allowed the aircraft's course to be more easily reconstructed as long as cloud cover did not substantially obscure the terrain. The early tracker camera carried 1,000ft of 70mm (2 3/8in x 9 1/2in) film recording an image roughly once every 32 seconds. The camera was usually turned on just after take-off to ensure it was not frozen before it reached operational altitudes. It weighed 58lb and used a 3.5-inch f/8 lens.

Early Main Cameras

The necessity for lightweight cameras saw new materials and novel design features which took time and effort to perfect. Renowned camera and lens designer James Baker initially used different combinations of old K-17 and K-38 cameras fitted with his newly designed Perkin-Elmer 24ins lens. This was an interim arrangement until his new camera design was ready.[9] The original A1 main camera arrangement used a 'rockable' K-38 (663lb) alternately swinging left and right of the camera's centreline. Although it produced good results the rocking mechanism was unreliable. Soon the A2 fit (675lb) which comprised three K-38s in a fan arrangement (vertical, right and left facing) with 24-inch f/8 lenses that used Kodak 9.5ins wide film became the most widely used. It carried an additional vertically mounted Perkin-Elmer tracking camera that used 70mm film to record the U-2's flight path.[10]

Clark company, to stop their blood from instantly boiling in an unpressurised environment.

The U-2's challenging handling qualities were soon reflected in serious losses. In addition to lots of minor mishaps, mostly on landing, aircraft and pilot fatalities grew too. Tables 7 and 8 (presented at the rear of this book) outline U-2A/C losses up to 1960 and reveal those losses were significant. Four U-2s in 1956. Five in 1957, including the programme's first fatal loss, with four more aircraft and two pilots lost in 1958. That meant nearly a quarter of the fleet had been written off and the repairable damage accidents placed additional pressures on airframe availability.

Sensors

To carry its photographic and – soon – electronic sensors at extreme altitudes required every effort be made to save weight and maximise its payload capacity. U-2 sensors faced two main constraints. First, the internal dimensions of the airframe limited the size of payload that could be carried within its equipment bay (Q-Bay). Approximately 67ins long, 55ins high and of varied internal widths, due to internal dimensions limitations of the fuselage. Second, the Q-Bay, on the U-2A, was limited to 500-750lb payload weight. When no payload was carried ballast weights had to be fitted.

Envisaged as a strategic photographic platform, huge efforts also went into developing specialised cameras with powerful lenses. They too were at the frontier of advanced technology. It soon

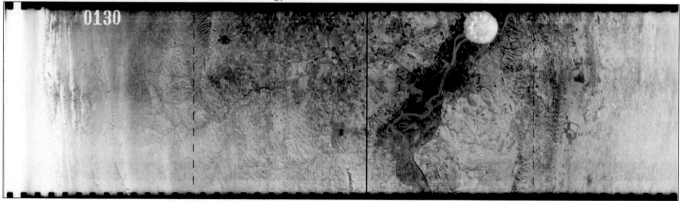

Tracking camera image from Mission 1554, 30 January 1960. This near horizon-to-horizon view is over the river Tigris in northern Iraq. The dark line indicates the centreline of the aircraft, the broken lines indicate the swath of territory covered by the B camera, when operated in Mode 2. The circle near the top of the shot is a clock stamp record of the image time. (NARA via Jason Ur).

Hycon 73 'B' Camera

Baker's new B camera arrived in 1956, a substantial leap forward in design and capability. Undertaking projects for both the USAF and Smithsonian Institute, Baker had effectively hidden his work in plain sight by not applying any special security restrictions to his U-2 work, in the hope that no one would notice this very secret project. The method was successful and considerably sped up the work.[11]

Like many advanced cameras designs, it initially experienced shutter function problems. Soon resolved, the B camera became the standard U-2 fit producing excellent results.[12] It was built around a Baker designed 36-inch f/10 lens that scanned from horizon-to-horizon with seven different imaging positions. This saved the weight of carrying multiple cameras. The lens was more powerful and so well produced that it generated very high-quality imagery with a resolution as small as 30ins from 65,000ft in ideal circumstances. A lighter version of the camera, the B2, was later developed and used into the 1970s.

The B camera had four modes of operation which could be switched in flight by the pilot:

- Mode 1: Up to 73.5 degrees left and right every 4.5 secs (10 positions, sequence V, 1R, 2L, 3L, 1L, V, 1R, 2R, 3R, 1L).
- Mode 2: 24.5 degrees left and right every 7.6 secs (3 positions, sequence: V, 1L, 1R)
- Mode 3: Right side only
- Mode 4: Left side only

The camera had seven different positions. Starting with the vertical, positions 1L and 1R were 24.5 degrees from the vertical. 2L and 2R were 49 degrees and 3L and 3R 73.5 degrees. These angles meant that the field of view from the 36-inch lens overlapped considerably. For positions 1L, V, 1R the overlap was sufficient to create high-quality stereographic images.

The lens positions 1L, 2L, 3L, V, 1R, 2R, 3R corresponded with ports on the underside of the U-2's equipment bay and the film was exposed using either a 1/150 or 1/300 of a second shutter speed. The 18ins square film format was created by exposing two 9.5x18ins strips of film simultaneously that ran in opposite directions across the camera's glass platten. This ensured that the weight distribution of the film from the two 6,000ft (later 6,500ft) film magazines did not disturb the U-2's centre of gravity or affect its control trim in

the air. However, the camera did miss objects exactly beneath the aircraft because of the small gap between the two film rolls.

Used in mode 2, it captured a swath of imagery approximately 8nm on each side of the aircraft. The highest resolution was obtained from the vertical shots, steadily reducing the further the image was from the vertical. Each shutter activation exposed one frame of film from each direction. Once processed the two images were matched together to produce up to 4,000 18ins square negatives. Each image negative was marked in the corner following the direction of flight,

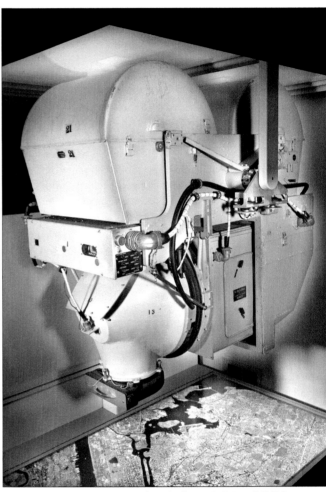

The B camera as it was mounted inside the U-2's Q-Bay. (NASM)

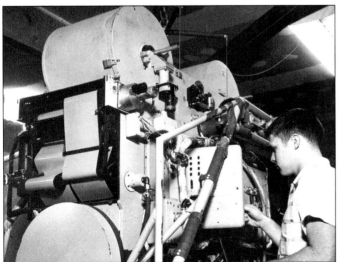

Bench testing a Hycon B camera, shows its inner workings. The film drums at the top spooled the film in opposite directions so that each image was composed of two 9.5x18ins negatives that were matched together after processing. (USAF)

The B camera's single lens took images from up to seven positions out of corresponding optical glass apertures on the underside of the fuselage. Every fifth frame was a vertical one, with those to the left and right angled at 24.5, 49 and 73.5 degrees each side of the vertical, labelled on the film as Left or Right 1, 2, 3 as appropriate. In the aft of the hatch, just behind those is a 'Dove prism' that gave the tracker camera horizon-to-horizon coverage. (NASM)

with a frame number and a clock indicating time, in the top and identified if it was the left or right half of the frame.

A proposed 'C' camera involved using an approximately 200ins focal length lens. Many-times more powerful than any existing equipment, James Baker discussed with Kelly Johnson the possibility of using a folded optics 240-inch lens. However, the payload space was just six inches short of the minimum size Baker could make the camera assembly, so it was abandoned. In March 1956 it was agreed that the 'C' camera would use a 144in f/16 lens producing 13x13in format negatives. That was revised when it was realised that a: 'Structural member interfered in allocated space.' As a consequence, the lens size was successively revised to be 144ins, then 120ins and finally up to 180ins. Art 343 was selected as the 'C' camera test vehicle and first flight tested on 21 December 1956. Flight trials continued through to November 1957. It experienced considerable problems with image focus and vibration. The camera was so powerful it took great effort to accurately aim.[13] The CIA's James Cunningham, then U-2 Administrative Officer and later a Deputy Director, Office of Special Activities explained: 'you had no sweep at all, if you happened to miss the target by 20ft you were out of luck; it was focussed that narrowly.'[14] On 28 March 1958 two CIA representatives visited Perkin-Elmer and reported the continued problems with the 'C' camera's development: 'around vibration and/or Image Movement Compensation.'[15] By 20 May 1958 abandonment of the 'C' camera saw Art 343 returned to a 'clean' configuration.[16] A 16 January 1959 CIA report lamented the cancellation of the 'C' camera at a time when the U-2 was increasingly being seen as a stand-off platform, where its ability to see deep into denied territory was potentially useful to validate simultaneously collected SIGINT data.[17]

Early SIGINT and Self-Protection Packages

The U-2 has come to be primarily regarded as a photographic platform, but throughout its career has been fitted with ever more sophisticated electronics. Some collected electronic Russian missile and radar signals (ELINT) with others targeting voice transmissions (COMINT). Different devices monitored the U-2's own systems performance and provided an element of self-protection. Collectively these were all known blandly as 'Systems' followed by a roman numeral for specific designation, a methodology intended to ensure security around individual items.[18]

Each System needed different antenna arrangements to detect the various signal bands, which were usually recorded for later exploitation. Each comprised several elements that had to be installed, often spread around different parts of the airframe. Only a few of each System were normally purchased. This meant the wiring required, brackets and electrical components necessary for each were usually installed in just a few specific airframes rather than fleet-wide. Some were done on-site, others required the return to the Lockheed works, or later, Edwards AFB. When Systems were installed operationally it was often found that electronic noise from existing equipment interfered with the new antenna or recorders. These problems had to be isolated and solutions devised, which could take considerable time. Some, like System V, were so bulky and heavy that the main mission camera had to be removed. The reel-to-reel tape recorders were initially very heavy and of dubious reliability. There were decisions to be made about activating them. Should they be switched on all the time? Should they be manually switched on, or could automatic activation be devised? How much tape could be carried to record the data? This equipment made considerable electrical power demands such that a separate generator was soon required.

Even when collection was successfully achieved, signal data exploitation was still in its infancy. CIA Deputy Assistant Director for Special Activities James Cunningham explained in a 1983 interview the difficulties faced with early ELINT operations: 'That was a world of experimentation, fuss and fidget with the damned systems, trying to optimise, and a lot of the time we got things that nobody knew what they were when we got them back. They'd say jeez, what the hell is that?'[19] The data had to be catalogued, its purpose identified and significance determined. For radars, it had to be successfully linked to specific types of Soviet equipment that were often difficult to identify because it was beyond photographic range.

Systems, Systems, Systems

Contractors Ramo-Wooldridge, later HRB-Singer and others were involved in designing and building these pioneering payloads in the early years. New generations replaced earlier variants, they became increasingly automated, extended the frequency ranges and used multitrack recorders. Critically they decreased in size and weight as electronics advanced.

System VI was a P, L, S and X-band combined COMINT/ELINT receiver used from 1959-66. Once described as a 'hodge podge installation' it suffered early on with significant problems from the cabling and junction boxes which caused excess noise and interference. In the original 1958 design proposal, as well as a ventral aerial two poor performing 'scimitar' or 'rams horn' were to be fitted too. (CIA, via Chris Pocock)

THE U-2'S FLEXIBLE SPINE

The U-2's upper fuselage soon became home to important equipment items. Some U-2s appeared with a small fuselage 'bump' behind the cockpit, roughly positioned above the wings. This housed an early Collins 180L-3 automatic HF antenna tuner for some of the onboard radio equipment.

System IXB 'false angle' projector, integrated with the System XIIB was developed by the Granger company from 1958. Intended to deceive Soviet X-band air intercept radars, it used a signal repeater to create 'false angles' attempting to convince the SAM's radar that the target was offset to one side of its actual position and so break the missile lock.

On the non-air refuelling equipped U-2Cs, System IXB was fitted in the specially developed pressurised 'long spine' that could accommodate up to 100lb loads, within which the equipment could be added and removed as required. It also housed the

Collins 618-T3 HF single sideband radio, navigation light and HF wire antenna to the tail.

The air refuelling equipped U-2E/U-2Fs had a much shorter 'hump' that housed the air refuelling receptacle with guide lighting, radio, RV beacon and antenna. (CIA)

Close up of a U-2C's full spine, gives a good indication of its dimensions. (MoA)

The air refuelling fairing of the U-2E/F housed the receptacle and associated equipment. (CIA)

U-2C N803X with the small hump housing the 180L-3 automatic tuner. (CIA)

U-2C N809X showing the full-length spine that housed the System IXB deception emitter and associated equipment. (CIA)

From the first operational flights in 1956 the Ramo-Wooldridge 'System I' was carried. It detected and recorded either S or X-band radar transmissions. Twelve sets of System I were purchased costing $309,600 and used from 1955-59.[20] The S or X-band selection had to be pre-set before take-off. The 10-hour tape recording capacity was usually turned on from the cockpit shortly after taking off. As early as 1955 System II was under development, intended to enable transmissions from U-2s in flight to base stations, using several pre-set messages comprising three-digit codes, best likened to a simple data link. However, the system was abandoned in 1956, never used operationally.[21] System III was a 44lb recorder to capture VHF air defence and ground control voice communications. It produced very poor quality results. COMINT was a low priority for Agency U-2 operations and was rapidly discontinued in 1957, although briefly resurrected in 1963.[22]

Taking more than two years to develop from 1955 'System IV' was an 'unattended airborne ferret' that used a 14-track tape recorder. It weighed 624lb and was carried on approximately 15 missions in the Baltic and Black Sea areas.[23] Fitted to U-2 Art 351 System IV listened in on Soviet communications associated with the launch of the Soviet 'Lunar 1' probe on January 2, 1959 (Mission 4019). System IV should have proved very valuable but suffered from serious electronic interference, caused by the U-2's own electrical equipment. There was a considerable effort to try and eliminate the noise, even with operational tests over the Black Sea, but the problems were never fully resolved.[24]

System V was the first solely ELINT payload. It was used from December 1956 for just three missions. It consisted of three, multitrack recorders and its specifically tuned receivers were tied to a number of frequency bands ranging from 60 to 10,750 megacycles. It was said to have functioned satisfactorily but it weighed over 400 pounds and so left no space for a main payload camera to be carried.[25] Short lived, it was replaced by the more versatile System VI.[26]

System VI was another Ramo-Wooldridge product. It replaced the ELINT and COMINT functions of Systems I, III and V and was built mainly of parts cannibalised from those older systems. It detected signals in the P, L, S and X-bands (using an antenna on each side of the aircraft) and recorded emissions from all four bands onto two, three-channel, tape recorders. It was small enough that the main camera could still be carried. Eighteen sets were procured with half still in use by 1966, having been modernised on at least two occasions. It too had initially suffered from internal electrical interference problems, but after new junction boxes and some rewiring, its performance was greatly improved. It was first successfully used in Art 367 at Detachment B from 1959.[27]

Designed by Haller-Raymond-Brown, System VII came into use during June 1959. It used an Ampex 814 Recorder, designed to automatically gather up to 12 minutes of data simultaneously from six different radio frequencies. This equipment used a distinctive 'rams horn' antenna. Just one example was funded, assembled by the end of 1958, tested at Edwards AFB then quickly sent to Turkey. It was used only by Det B, for approximately 23 flights during 1959-60. It was intended to collect missile and rocket telemetry as they were launched from Plesetsk, Kapustin Yar in southern Russia or Sary Shagan in Eastern Kazakhstan.[28] Then advanced technology, System VII also experienced problems with internal system noise, sensitivity, range, automatic activation and recording quality issues. Even when it worked launch data would often be only partially recorded and was not always of decipherable quality.

The U-2's increasing vulnerability to improving Soviet air defences soon saw greater emphasis on electronic defensive and self-reporting systems. Developed by Granger from 1958, System IX was an important piece of self-protection equipment. It was used to deceive Soviet X-band air intercept radars. It used a signal repeater to create 'false angles' convincing the radar that the target was to one side of where it was so hoping to break the missiles lock. It was carried on Gary Powers' aircraft when he was shot down on 1 May 1960. Subsequently, redesigned and improved System IXA was trialled in Art 356 from May 1963 and later modifications took it to the System IXD version.[29]

After the 1960 debacle even more effort was put into developing electronic defensive equipment for the U-2 which were soon pressed into service. System XII was built from 1962 with 15 sets delivered by March 1963. It alerted the U-2 pilot when his aircraft was illuminated by the SA-2 SAM's 'Fan Song' radars. It became more sophisticated with successive updates able to indicate range and bearing. Sanders Associates in 1963 began with 'System XIIIA' using parts of the ALQ-19 jammer, intended to defeat SA-2 fire control radars. Part of the equipment was installed in the slipper tanks and became very important for Det H U-2 operations from Taiwan. Similarly, 'System XIV' (the ALQ-49) and 'System XV' (the ALQ-51) were countermeasures, used by the USAF as well as the CIA, also intended to be effective against the SA-2's 'Fan Song' radar. The latter was a very effective system and additionally procured for the SR-71, RB-57 and Air Force U-2s. From February 1965 the Oscar Sierra (Oh-Shit) System used a passive detector that turned on a cockpit warning light when it detected an enemy missile guidance signal within 40 miles, turning on the 'System XIII' jammers and alerting the 'Birdwatcher' system. Birdwatcher periodically collected data on the U-2's in-flight performance (altitude, exhaust temperature and more) then sent in a burst transmission. It was used to help establish possible explanations in the event of a U-2 loss. From 1967–68 'System XX' used an infra-red sensor intended to detect the engine heat signatures from pursuing enemy aircraft.[30] Whilst the effectiveness of all these systems can sometimes be questioned, they pioneered many elements of early ELINT collection and the later development of electronic defensive countermeasures.

Aircraft and Equipment Modifications

The CIA's U-2 fleet was in a constant state of flux. They were being continuously updated, new equipment added and older, or poorer performing equipment, removed. There was no single 'standard' or modification fit. This posed significant challenges for U-2 engineers. As well as the constant modification work, there was routine maintenance and engineering issues arising from its unique design and the demands placed upon the airframe. SAC aircraft were not modified in the same way, or to the same extent, so their U-2s were again of different equipment standards, mostly not as well equipped as Agency aircraft. Of the 55 early U-2s built for the CIA (20) and SAC (35), all but a handful were eventually lost in training accidents or operations.

Almost everything about the U-2 was unique. Its basic design, its operating altitudes, its ground-breaking optical and electronic sensor payloads. It should also be remembered that the work was mostly undertaken in those early years not by CIA staff but by Lockheed and the various specialist equipment manufacturers like Ramo-Wooldridge, HRB etc. Whilst early testing and development took place in the US, once aircraft deployed overseas the maintenance complications grew dramatically. The considerable contribution of the often civilian contractors, technicians and flight mechanics to the U-2's success often gets missed.

Table 1: Basic U-2 Equipment Fits, February 1959[†]		
Equipment fit	No	Article No.
Photographic	14	347, 348, 356, 362, 363, 370, 373, 374, 379, 388, 390, 391, 392, 393
Sampling	6	372 (prototype), 381, 382, 383, 384, 385
APQ-56	3	350, 375, 395
ASN-6	3	376, 386, 387
Test/Training	13	342, 343, 344, 349, 351, 352, 353, 355, 358, 359, 360, 367, 378, 394[*]
U-2s lost prior to February 1959		341, 345, 346, 354, 357, 361, 364, 365, 366, 368, 369, 371, 377, 380, 389 (15 aircraft)
Source: [†] U-2 *Utility Flight Handbook*, 1959, Sections 5-17/5-18 [*] Art 394 was the first two-seat aircraft.		

There was the regular aircraft rotation to Lockheed for scheduled maintenance, testing and new equipment installation. There were constant service bulletins (SBs) to be implemented on the aircraft. Some had to be done in the US, many others were managed in the field. Some were relatively straightforward, others necessitated major engineering. Of course, it was not just the installation of new equipment itself that had to be done. All the wiring, fixing brackets and frames had to be installed too, and any controls required installed in the cockpit. Although separate, the cameras' systems were another major, complex piece of technology that required constant attention and modification.

The CIA's *U-2 Utility Flight Handbook*, gives a detailed insight of the modification states and different main equipment fits for all the early CIA and USAF U-2 airframes in 1959. At its simplest, all the aircraft could be configured to fulfil all the roles assigned to the U-2. However, as more specialist equipment became available and was installed into individual aircraft, it became more complex and time-consuming to configure them with very different main payloads. So, for example, U-2 Art 372 was primarily configured for the fallout sampling role (F-2 and P-2 equipment – see below). It could not carry the APQ-56 or ASN-6 navigation equipment at the same time. The combined sampler equipment weighed 799lb, the APQ-56/ASN-6 combinations weighed upward of 569lb and 341lb respectively and anyway could not both be physically accommodated together in the aircraft equipment bay behind the cockpit.[31] Table 1 shows the principal equipment 'roles' assigned to individual aircraft in February 1959.

Photographic Fit

As mentioned earlier, by 1959 two main types of camera were in use. Each required a different hatch bay cover through which images were shot. The aircraft were also fitted with a Mk III drift sight, sextant, tracker camera, plus System I and III, and the KWM-1 High Frequency transceiver. It was the U-2s configured primarily for photographic tasks that bore the brunt of operational work and allowed others to be used for continued trials and equipment testing back in the continental US.

Fallout Sampling

Responsibility for radioactive monitoring flights was initially a CIA one and they continued to periodically conduct covert missions when required. Art 372 served as the prototype for the collection system. From 1957–63 the USAF High Altitude Sampling Programme (HASP), often known as 'Crowflight' became the public face of U-2 operations. Five U-2s (Arts 381–385) were fitted with the 'Armed Forces Special Weapons Project' (AFSWP) 'hard nose.' These were mostly flown by SAC pilots. The USAF aircraft operated from many

locations for these missions including: RAF Upper Heyford, East Sale in Australia, Alaska and Ramey AFB, Puerto Rico. Their 'ownership' was made obvious by the application of large US Air Force titles and markings. They fulfilled that role until the agreement to halt above-ground nuclear testing entered into force in 1963. After that the obvious need for such missions declined significantly, although the CIA maintained a limited covert capability.[32]

These aircraft used a 'particulate atmospheric sampler' to collect high altitude nuclear fallout. Samples were collected on a series of six 16ins diameter filter papers. The 'F-2 Foil' equipment required a special hatch installation mounted on the lower opening of the Q-Bay. The filters were rotated into and out of the sampling position. When a filter was in place, its exposure was controlled by a door in the air inlet duct. The door was opened by an electric actuator allowing outside air to be ducted in, passed through the filter and expelled.[33] An 'automatic observer' in the Q-Bay photographed a repeated display of cockpit indicator lights, plus a duplicate altimeter reading, outside air temperature reading and clock every 15 seconds.[34] Once a filter paper exposure was completed the next cycled into position. The F-2 package weighed 171lb.

The frame mounted A2 camera fan arrangement was placed beneath the U-2's Q-Bay and winched into position. (Lockheed Martin)

The P-2 fallout sampling equipment required a special hatch and externally mounted air sampler beneath the Q-bay. (USAF Museum)

form of a digital readout from 70° north to 70° south… A PC-204A RADAN system is used in conjunction with the ASN-6 installation in order to provide the necessary drift angle and ground speed information to the ASN-6 computer.'[40] The ASN-6 and associated equipment weighed 1041lb.

These early RADAN systems struggled in prolonged operation over smooth water. Successful integration of the systems proved too much and, as Chris Pocock noted, the ASN-6 system never worked well.[41] Though not used operationally they provided knowledge that aided the development, and later success of such equipment.

The associated P-2 Platform, weighed 411lb, was used to collect and store air samples and could only be used in conjunction with the F-2 system. The air samples were compressed to 2,300 PSI and stored in six spherical shatterproof bottles, each 13ins in diameter. The air was compressed by three 'Rootes blowers' and a four-stage compressor.[35]

It was later discovered that the two different sampling systems collected fallout at different rates. From June 1959 several missions used both nose and hatch samplers and showed a disparity in the readings detected. In 1960 further tests from Edwards AFB enabled the collection rates to be accurately recalculated. These indicated that the payload bay P-2 system collected around 2.5 times more activity than the hard nosed aircraft did.[36]

APQ-56

Three aircraft were provided with APQ-56 radars. Proposed in 1955, this K-band system was a mapping set, an early sideways looking radar system. Using a double antenna it scanned both sides of the aircraft and had a small cockpit monitoring screen with the recorder carried in the Q-Bay. This and the associated payload package, including the PC-210A RADAN (Radar Doppler Automatic Navigation) associated with use of the APQ-56, weighed 917lb. The imagery was clearly of low quality, described by the Ad-hoc Requirements Committee (ARC) as 'much inferior' but it could see through cloud.[37] Although tested, it was not used operationally. It was not cheap and an invoice prices a single set at $13,276 in 1959.[38] It was a very early forerunner to the much more sophisticated ASARS systems installed in the SR-71, and TR-1/U-2 in the late Cold War.[39]

RADAN, AN/ASN-6

High precision navigation over long distances was essential for U-2 missions, to ensure accurate positioning for overhead photography and peripheral SIGINT missions. Until such a system was developed navigation was entirely reliant on visual means.

The AN/ASN-6 was described as a: 'Latitude and longitude computer,' used to establish the U-2's position. It 'continuously computes and displays the aircraft's latitude and longitude in the

Test and Training

This is a slightly arbitrary 'catch all' category. Most of the U-2s in this group were used over the years for pilot training, or as equipment test aircraft at Edwards AFB. The latter were mostly one-off test fits, that then sometimes saw brief operational evaluation with Detachments. For example, Art 344 carried the sole System VII equipment used for 'missile chasing.' It was converted in 1959 sent to Detachment B at Adana. When Detachment B was withdrawn it returned to Edwards AFB and the equipment was removed.[42] For another example Art 343 was committed to trials associated with the powerful 'C' camera.

Weather Packages

A significant amount of time and money was expended in developing weather reconnaissance packages for the U-2. Three Weather Packages were built for installation in the U-2's equipment bay. They consisted of: 'instrumentation to measure and record airspeed, altitude, free air temperature, humidity, acceleration, time and aircraft heading.'[43] The total package weighed 747lb.[44] Although producing some useful high altitude meteorological data they were essentially used to provide legitimate cover for more covert operations.

A superficial examination of weather reconnaissance sorties suggests these missions were largely for training purposes, to test the integration of new navigation equipment in particular. A meeting on 1 May 1959 with the CIA's 'Material Branch,' included an Air Weather Service representative. He indicated that the meteorological value of the early WP packages was close to zero.[45] In November 1957 the CIA purchased four PC-211 RADAN systems for integration with the three Weather Packages (WPs).[46] These were plagued with problems and frequently failed.

Detachment B used this equipment during 1959 on several operations. Art 349 was used for British weather flights from RAF Watton in May and October 1959 (see Chapter 3). Mission records show six similar missions were launched by Det B from Adana in March and April 1959 installed in Arts. 349, 351 and 367 over the Mediterranean. From Astugi, Det C also flew six weather missions from 27 March to 24 April 1959, with a WP installed in

THE APQ-56

The APQ-56 was an early sideways looking radar system, primarily intended for navigational use when cloud undercast prevented the pilot seeing the ground. A complex piece of equipment to operate, it collected data 15 miles each side of the U-2 up to 70,000ft. A 70mm camera was used to record a continuously moving filmstrip with a tiny cockpit repeater screen.

Cockpit control unit for APQ-56. (National Electronics Museum)

Fig. . AN/APQ 56 Radar Image of an Area on the Seward Peninsula, Alaska. U.S. Air Force Photograph.

Imagery from the APQ-56 was of poor quality compared to conventional photography and at its most useful along coasts to distinguish between land and sea. (CIA)

Data recorder for the APQ-56 (right). The tiny green visual monitor screen in the cockpit must have been next to useless to the pilot (left). (National Electronics Museum)

The film processing storage unit for the APQ-56. (National Electronics Museum)

Art 353. Similar to the flights in Europe these missions were pretty perfunctory cover operations. Of greater interest were the four typhoon hunting missions flown from Astugi between 14 July to 25 September 1958. Their ability to fly high 'above' these systems produced some spectacular early typhoon photography as the first aircraft ever to able to fly above these systems to photograph them.[47]

It was without doubt Kelly Johnson's remarkable design of the U-2 that made it possible to enter into service so quickly and undertake overflights of the USSR from 1956-60. Equipped with remarkable cameras and improving electronics it became a formidable multi-sensor platform. The need for photographic operations was particularly urgent to collect as much overhead intelligence as possible before Soviet air defences finally closed the 'window' of opportunity and successfully shoot them down. In the following chapters we look in some detail at how those early operations were carried out.

2
ABOVE AND BEYOND

For maximum gain the U-2 had to begin operations rapidly, which meant passing a significant number of milestones. First was testing and proving of the aircraft and its equipment and incorporating any subsequent modifications required. Pilots, or in CIA parlance 'Drivers,' had to be selected and trained, as did engineers and ground crews. Overseas basing arrangements had to be in place before operational flights could begin. Those were major, complex, tasks to be accomplished in the utmost secrecy and get photographic results before Soviet air defences were able to reach up and bring a U-2 down. Time was short.

First Operational Deployment
In January 1956, Richard Bissell sought, through simultaneous approaches to the RAF and MI6, to operate the U-2 from the UK for an initial series of overflights. In return for basing the US would share the photographic 'take' in line with previously agreed intelligence sharing agreements.[1] Permission was given to use the US Air Force base at RAF Lakenheath, to be known as 'Detachment A'.

By 7 May 1956 the first U-2s and their support personnel had arrived at Lakenheath courtesy of 11 C-124s and two C-118 flights.[2] Just before the first operations politics intervened. Royal Navy Commander Lionel 'Buster' Crabb died in a failed Secret Intelligence Service (SIS) sponsored diving operation on the Soviet cruiser 'Ordjoninkidze,' moored in Portsmouth harbour for a goodwill visit. Much of the political scandal was subsequently played out in the British national press and the Head of SIS sacked. Prime Minister Anthony Eden requested Eisenhower postpone U-2 flights from Britain. The Americans rapidly switched preparations to Wiesbaden in West Germany. Wiesbaden was a very busy airfield, believed to be closely watched by Soviet agents. On the positive side, it was next to USAFE's main intelligence and photo processing units. Det A later moved to specially renovated facilities at Giebelstadt Air Base in October 1956, but that was used for just four operational missions before it too was abandoned.

The First Few Flights
Detachment 'A' with four U-2As moved to Wiesbaden on 11 June 1956 where the aircraft were immediately retrofitted with more powerful J-57/P-31 engines. These were less susceptible to flameouts than the earlier version. Operations needed to get underway quickly to maximise the spring clear air and good photographic weather. Eisenhower, still hesitant about authorising the first overflights, accepted further assurances that even if detected the U-2s were unlikely to be tracked and if downed probably not traced back to the US.[3]

USAFE had planned 16 overflights starting in June 1956, using modified 'Heart Throb' B-57s and 'Slick Chick' RF-100As. Joint Chiefs of Staff authority for these missions was already granted to: 'obtain intelligence on SACEURs Atomic Strike List.'[4] As flight authorisations were already in place HQ USAF and USAFE willingly supported the CIA missions. The U-2s at Wiesbaden adroitly took over the scheduled USAFE mission programme. Covering the same target list, it was accomplished with far fewer flights than the original USAF plan required.[5]

The immediate priorities for U-2 overflights were determined by the Committee on Requirements (COMOR), limited by its approximately 3,400-mile maximum range. These were:

1. Long-range Soviet bomber bases
2. Air defences
3. Atomic energy installations
4. Guided missile installations
5. Naval bases and shipyards
6. Industrial complexes
7. Dispositions and capabilities of military forces[6]

The first three U-2 flights over Eastern Europe were not really of sufficient importance to justify U-2 use but were a valuable 'shakedown' opportunity before venturing over the Soviet Union. The first, Mission 2003, on 20 June 1956 covered Polish, East German and Czechoslovak targets. It was followed by two more flights on 2 July 1956. On 21 June Eisenhower had approved a series of deep penetration overflights of the USSR for rapid completion. This was slightly delayed following Nikita Khrushchev's invitation to USAF CinC General Nathan Twining to visit Moscow. Eisenhower gave final approval for a 10-day period of Soviet overflights from 4 July.

Table 2: Initial Detachment A flights, 1956 with A2 camera fit

Date	Msn	Pilot	Countries overflown
20 June	2003	Overstreet	Poland.
2 July	2009	Dunaway	Hungary, Czechoslovakia, Bulgaria, Romania incursion into Yugoslavia due to cloud. A camera failure.
2 July	2010	Kratt	GDR, Romania, Hungary, Poland.
4 July	2013	Stockman	Poland, USSR (Leningrad, Tallinn, Riga). Partial camera failure.

5 July	2014	Vito	GDR, Poland, USSR (Minsk, Moscow, Ivanovo, Kalinin).
9 July	2020	Knutson	Poland, USSR.
9 July	2021	Overstreet	Hungary, USSR, Poland, Czechoslovakia.
10 July	2023	Dunaway	GDR, Poland, USST (Belarus, Ukraine) Romania, Hungary, Czechoslovakia.

Whilst regarded as successful missions, there were technical problems associated with most flights too. On Missions 2009, 2010, 2013 and 2020 there were shutter failures on the oblique A2 cameras rendering the film unusable and there were hatch fogging issues on some flights (2010, 2013 for example). Photographic hatches covered the lower equipment bay, each designed to match different camera and SIGINT equipment fits. The hatches were near unique to each different fit. The camera equipment bay was electrically heated to prevent moisture collecting and causing lens fogging.

Weather over the U-2's route always presented challenges that multiplied on deep penetration flights. Cloud cover prevented photography and seriously hindered accurate navigation. Stronger than forecast high-level winds could adversely affected the U-2's range and for some planned long-distance missions there was a real risk of running out of fuel.

Mission 2023

One of the most comprehensive reports publicly available from that first group of flights covers Mission 2023. This was flown by Det A pilot Glen Dunaway from Wiesbaden on 10 July 1956. He took off in darkness at 0331Z hrs using the U-2A marked as 'NACA 163.' Dunaway's U-2 carried an A2 and tracking camera fit. On 2023 the first 200ft of tracker film was useless, hopelessly underexposed

having taken off well before dawn. Penetration of GDR airspace was at 65,000ft and Dunaway passed 27 navigational waypoints where his U-2 changed course. The turn points were mostly selected to maximise the main camera's coverage of priority targets. As the fuel burned off the aircraft became lighter, slowly climbed and reached a maximum height of 68,000ft. The flight progressed over the GDR, then Poland, into Soviet Ukraine, over the Black Sea, returning via Romania, Hungary, Czechoslovakia and the GDR again.[7] Near Lviv, Dunaway passed close to Stryy airfield. Unknown to him on its south-western edge was an early 'special weapons' storage area. His 2042-mile round trip arrived back at Wiesbaden at 1206Z, airborne for 8hrs 35mins and recorded nearly 100 targets.

Soviet Protests

After this initial series of U-2 missions on 10 July 1956 a Soviet protest was delivered to the US State Department by Soviet Ambassador Georgi Zaroubin. He described American 'gross violations of Soviet airspace' on 4, 5 and 9 July. They seemed to initially believe these missions were flown by a 'twin engined' aircraft, probably thinking they were 'Heart Throb' RB-57As that had previously overflown satellite states.[10] Seemingly by chance, but perhaps not, James Killian, Director of the Technological Capabilities Panel, was visiting an NSA ground listening post in Germany on 4 July 1956 when he heard the US operators listening into unusual chatter over the Soviet air defence network. The NSA staff were puzzled that the Soviet transmissions mentioned an aircraft flying at an 'abnormally high altitude' as they tried to identify what it was. From that time at least, very senior personnel at the apex of U-2 operations knew that its activities were being 'seen' by the Soviets, even if only intermittently.[11]

Polish and Czech government protests soon followed. Given that previous 'Slick Chick' RF-100A and 'Heart Throb' RB-57 missions had been detected, and tracked, the Americans appeared surprised

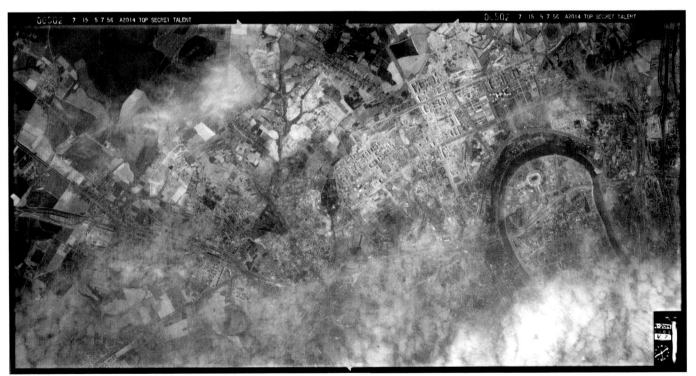

Mission 2014, 5 July 1956, climbed westerly after taking off from Wiesbaden until it reached 60,000ft over Belgium and then turned eastwards to enter GDR airspace at 64,000ft. As it passed over the south-eastern edge of Moscow at 0708Z it was at 65,000ft. In the loop of the River Moskva is the Lizhniki (Central Lenin) Stadium, in the final stages of construction, opened on 31 July 1956, just a few weeks before the image was taken. On the opposite bank of the Moskva is Moscow State University. This flight also captured images of Fili airfield, close to central Moscow. This frame from the A2 camera had a ground coverage of 8x4 nm. (NARA via Lin Xu and Chris Pocock)

STRYY 'SPECIAL WEAPONS AREA'[8]

Flying close to Lviv in western Ukraine on July 10, 1956, Mission 2023 identified Stryy airfield, a few miles to the southwest of the town. Just two images taken by its A2 camera revealed an early nuclear storage site, for a small number of tactical weapons. Most references to nuclear weapons and sites remain redacted from declassified CIA reports. But by piecing together some tiny fragments of information it is possible to get an insight into just what it was possible to discern from this early overhead U-2 imagery. Careful analysis of the two images allowed detailed drawings of the site to be constructed.

They identify the storage site, buildings and parts of the facility labelled, including earth mounds, entry gates and so on. Many even have approximate dimensions. When compared to recent satellite imagery, many of the abandoned sites basic features are still discernible. It is a clear demonstration of the Agency PIs' professional skills in 1956, that they could derive such details from U-2 imagery. Although far from complete, it is clear that significant details of these 'special weapons' storage areas were discernible. The available aerial imagery would have been supplemented by 'other source' intelligence, in this case, two brief 1959-60 CIA reports mention the use of external labour shipped in to undertake some high security 'continuous excavation and construction work.' Another indicates construction of an 'underground hangar' – probably the main storage bays for nuclear components – which required special passes to access.

Images of similar sites allowed intelligence agencies to identify the evolving designs of these nuclear storage bunkers. Included in the early analyses were facilities at Baranovichi, Bobruysk, Bykhov, Orsha and Siauliai airfields all in various stages of construction. Early nuclear weapons' stores were often located four-to-six miles away from the airfields, connected by hard-surfaced roads and served by taxiways from the runways. A second design style was noted at Karankut, Minsk, Soltsy and Stryy that placed the special weapons' stores much closer, adjacent to the airfield. These locations were repeat targeted by later U-2 flights whenever possible. The arrival of satellite imagery from 1960, and its rapid improvement, allowed detailed 'target' folders to be constructed of such sites, charting changes from earlier imagery.

Dunaway's U-2A was fitted with Systems I and III. Positioned in the nose cone, System I recorded X or S-band radar transmissions. System III recorded VHF communications, also fixed in the nose. Both were turned on shortly after take-off. The recorders were logged as turned on at 0334Z and both functioned normally. During the mission, the System I's S-band aerials detected 158 different signals from the left side of the aircraft and a further 146 from the right. From the signal type, strength, directions and examining the time indicators on the tapes, it was possible for analysts to plot the origin of individual signals and determine what many of them were (height finding, GCI, SAM, intercept radars etc). Soviet Token (P-20 'Periskop') early warning radar signals were reported to have been almost continuously monitored the U-2, on occasion by up to eight sets simultaneously. Gun-laying radars were detected eight times including west of Lviv and on the Crimean peninsula.

Attached to the mission report is some intriguing additional material. It contains details from the debriefing of someone simply identified as 'DS–727', a

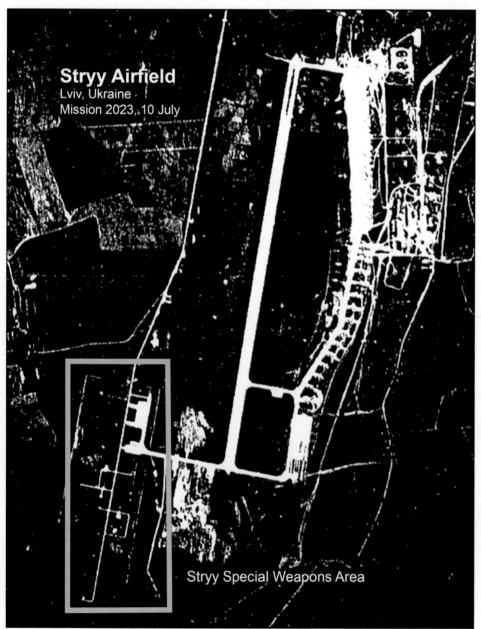

Stryy Airfield
Lviv, Ukraine
Mission 2023, 10 July

Stryy Special Weapons Area

Basic image of Stryy airfield taken by Mission 2023. Special weapons area highlighted. (CIA)

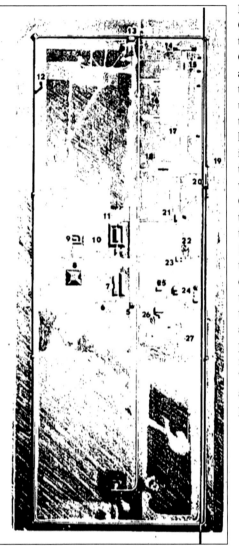

1. REVETTED PARKING APRON 42 X 42 FEET.

2. WOODEN FENCE WITH GUARD TOWERS AT THE CORNERS AND AT INTERVALS ALONG THE LONGER SIDES. FENCE, 4300 X 1500 FEET, ENCLOSES AN AREA OF 148 ACRES.

3. POSSIBLE WIRE FENCE.

4. MAIN ROAD WITHIN INSTALLATION 21 FEET WIDE.

5. PROBABLE EARTH-COVERED BUILDING 21 X 32 FEET.

6. INNER FENCED AREA 570 X 815 FEET. THREE SMALL BUILDINGS ARE LOCATED ADJACENT TO FENCE.

7. H-SHAPED DRIVE-THROUGH BUILDING WITH 42 X 54 FOOT WINGS AND 32 X 58 FOOT CENTER SECTION. A LARGE EARTH REVETMENT IS LOCATED ALONGSIDE THE BUILDING ON THE SIDE NEAREST THE AIRFIELD. THIS BUILDING COULD POSSIBLY BE USED AS AN ASSEMBLY BUILDING FOR COMPONENTS OF A NUCLEAR BOMB OR A MISSILE.

8. EARTH-COVERED, FLAT-TOPPED, PYRAMIDAL-SHAPED BUNKER 117 X 128 FEET. A 10 FOOT ACCESS ROAD LEADS TO SMALL ENTRANCES ON EITHER SIDE OF THE BUNKER. THIS BUNKER COULD POSSIBLY BE USED FOR STORAGE OF NUCLEAR COMPONENTS OF A NUCLEAR BOMB OR FOR THE WARHEAD OF A MISSILE.

9. REVETTED BUILDING 21 X 23 FEET.

10. MOUND 21 X 21 FEET. (POSSIBLE EARTH COVERED BUILDING.

11. REVETTED BUILDING 43 X 120 FEET, WITH ACCESS ROADS ENTERING REVETMENT AT BOTH ENDS. ON ONE END OF REVETMENT IS A PARKING APRON 53 X 75 FEET. ON THE OTHER END IS AN ASSOCIATED SMALL BUILDING, 21 X 42 FEET.

12. CIRCULAR TOWER WITH CYLINDRICAL TOP.

13. PROBABLE GUARD HOUSE AT ROAD GATE.

14. BLAST WALL.

15. LOADING RAMP 60 X 160 FEET; RAMP NARROWS TO 55 FEET AT REAR; WITH LOADING PIT 10 X 60 FEET.

16. LOADING RAMPS 62 X 120 FEET; RAMPS NARROW TO 50 FEET AT REAR; WITH LOADING PITS 10 X 60 FEET.

17. SERVICING APRON 220 X 490 FEET.

18. LARGE LOADING RAMP 140 X 330 FEET WITH LOADING PIT 10 X 70 FEET. LOADING PIT WIDENS SLIGHTLY NEAR CENTER.

19. TAXIWAY GATE. A TAXIWAY, 70 FEET WIDE, EXTENDING FROM THE RUNWAY ENTERS THROUGH THIS GATE.

20. PROBABLE GATE CONTROL HOUSE.

21. BUILDING 30 X 55 FEET.

22. ROAD 10 FEET WIDE.

23. BUILDING 30 X 30 FEET.

24. BUILDING 32 X 42 FEET.

25. BUILDING 21 X 53 FEET; PARKING APRON IN FRONT OF BUILDING MEASURES 42 X 53 FEET.

26. BUILDING 42 X 88 FEET WITH 28 FOOT PARKING APRON. L-SHAPED STRUCTURE WITH WINGS MEASURING 23 X 42 FEET AND 23 X 53 FEET PROJECTS FROM REAR OF BUILDING.

27. ROAD 16 FEET WIDE.

NOTE: ALL MEASUREMENTS ARE APPROXIMATE.

MEASUREMENTS SOMEWHAT LESS RELIABLE THAN THE REST DUE TO POOR IMAGE AT THESE POINTS.

Hungarian Observer and Control Officer, formerly of the 99th Fighter Division Control Centre at Taszár airfield. He had escaped to Austria during the later uprising, a few months after this flight. DS–727 described how a Hungarian-Russian interpreter was on duty at all times and when their airspace was penetrated the Centre's Observer Officer would guide the interceptor towards the target. On this occasion: 'The [Soviet] MiG-19 pilot reported that he had reached an altitude of 18,000 metres and was unable to climb any higher, the height of the penetrating aircraft was estimated by the pilot at 20,000 metres.'[9] The record for Mission 2023 states: 'Intercept attempt by Farmer a/c near Bacau, Romania' but provides no further detail.

From U-2 images detailed drawings of buildings and features at key locations would be made, often with approximate dimensions. (CIA)

Stryy airfield and abandoned special weapons area today. (Maxar, CNES/Airbus)

that U-2 flights were accurately monitored. Quite why the U-2's detection by Soviet and satellite air defences should have come as a surprise to Eisenhower is rather odd. US beliefs that the Soviets would be unable to track the U-2 were based on earlier flight tests conducted in the US, where their radars were unable to consistently detect and track them. It appears to have been largely assumed that as the US radars were not totally successful neither would be the Soviets'.

Further flights were immediately halted, with the instruction passed to Richard Bissell by White House Chief of Staff General Andrew Goodpaster. It saw a marked decline in Eisenhower's long-term enthusiasm for the U-2.[12] The halt meant Detachment A in Germany now had little further operational value and marked the start of its decline. It conducted no further Soviet overflights.

Managing a Strategic Reconnaissance Programme

The rapid growth in intrusive US intelligence gathering activities brought increased centralised control and coordination. Those efforts included: US Navy ships, submarines and aircraft, CIA U-2s, USAF RB-47, RB-57 missions and an expanding peripheral flight programme. The operations required political authorisation for broad policy and targeting. At the military level operations required detailed planning and careful coordination to ensure their smooth running.

President Eisenhower was directly involved in authorising these initial U-2 flights. An indication of how overflights (not just CIA ones) were approved is outlined in an Agency memo from 30 October 1953. The procedure required establishing a military need for the imagery, securing agreement from the Joint Chiefs, the Secretary of Defence with concurrence from the Department of State and the CIA Director. For the formal process the memo explains 'a decision [was taken] by the President that he did not wish to be involved in the approval of overflights, because of the implications of Executive concurrence in the event that any overflights were intercepted or that operational failure took place.'[13]

However, we are presented with conflicting accounts of just how involved Eisenhower really was in the U-2 operations. Some sources have attempted to distance him from the process, whilst others have described him as having direct, detailed involvement down to modifying individual mission routes. Mission planning and implementation were further complicated by Eisenhower's periods of serious illness and hospitalisation around that time. These meant his oversight and control of operations was probably not always as he would have wanted it to be.

To make the U-2 programme happen quickly, before the opportunity for overflights of the USSR disappeared, Eisenhower had deliberately pushed the lead responsibility to the CIA. It was a much more agile organisation than the Air Force, riven with its complex and often competing command structure. At the same time, he was concerned about the CIA's high degree of autonomy in the covert action field. The two needed to be balanced.

Eisenhower approved National Security Council (NSC) circular 5412 on 15 March 1954 in part to institutionalise political control over U-2 operations. This made the Director of Central Intelligence (DCI) responsible for coordinating with representatives from State and Defence Departments to ensure that covert operations were 'planned and conducted in a manner consistent with US foreign and military policies.' The DCI exercised discretion in what proposals were considered by this 'Special Group 5412,' or simply 'Special Group.' Its composition varied, dependent on the topic addressed. In

1957 the Chairman of the JCS joined the Group. Meetings appear to have been infrequent until 1959 when weekly sessions commenced.[14]

A 'special meeting' in the President's Office at the White House on 18 January 1957 included the Vice President, Secretary of State, Director CIA, Chairman JCS, National Security Council Representative and others to address the topic of political deniability. Eisenhower raised the point: 'that there were some things which came up in the NSC 5412 field which it was better that the President and Secretaries should not know about so that they could be in a position to disavow them if necessary.' He further added that whilst it was right that he, or one of the other major principals should be consulted on the sensibility of a proposal and be aware of the project, it was also important that they did not know details of these programmes.[15]

Whilst the Special Group process was designed to insulate the President from the fallout of any disaster, it was frequently not adhered to. Andrew Goodpastor has indicated that Eisenhower still gave approval to every individual U-2 overflight of the USSR.[16] Michael Beschloss has asserted that the President felt that 'spy flights [were] too sensitive for consideration even by the Special Group.'[17] He had to balance the possible intelligence gain from these overflights, against the risks of reputation, perhaps even war, if the US was proved to be flying them. Exactly how much Eisenhower knew about some individual flights was described by Richard Bissell in a later interview. He explained that after the Intelligence Board and Ad-hoc Requirements Committee (ARC) designated specific targets, these were marked up on a map identifying individual locations and other details. Almost invariably Bissell, Allen Dulles and Cabell for the CIA, Foster Dulles, or his deputy, from the State Department and Chairman of the JCS were asked to brief the President. Eisenhower:

> [We] would run through this. At the end, the President would ask a lot of questions and as a 'general rule,' it came more and more to be his habit that he would let us go and give us his decision through Goodpastor a day or so later. However, he would always get the map on his desk and look at it, and always ask me to come around and explain this or that feature of it, and there were some occasions, more than once, when he would say, "well you can go there, but I want you to leave out that leg and go straight that way. I want you to go from B to D because it looks like you might be getting a little exposed over here," or something of that kind.[18]

From A to B

Following the suspension of penetration missions over Eastern Europe and the USSR from Wiesbaden, Detachment A's work came to a near halt. It needed new tasks. Even in those first few overflights the U-2 had proved its capabilities. It had managed to safely cross Eastern Europe on multiple occasions, then some of the most heavily defended airspace in the world, and even reached Moscow. Those first five Soviet penetration flights substantially met their primary objective covering nine of Soviet Long Range Aviation's main bomber bases. They revealed that the feared Soviet 'Bison' were not present at all, let alone in substantial numbers. This was far from the feared modern, nuclear-capable bomber fleet they thought they might find. The flights very quickly disproved the 'bomber gap' theory, then causing much public concern and congressional hysteria in the US.[19]

Operations continued from Wiesbaden for a while, with 11 missions over southern Europe and the Middle East. On 29 August 1956 two U-2s covered the eastern Mediterranean monitoring the

Anglo-French build-up for the forthcoming Suez invasion. Some flights fuel-stopped at Adana in Turkey. They quickly brought the U-2 into the middle of a simmering international conflict. The flights covered a range of targets in Sicily, Italy, France, Egypt, Israel, Jordan, Lebanon, Malta, Cyprus and Syria. At least some of that imagery, especially of Egypt, was shared with the British at a London meeting on 7 September 1956, encouraged by ARC chairman James Reber and PID Head Art Lundahl. It included photography covering the Canal zone taken on 30 August.[20] Eventually Eisenhower, exasperated with the continued Anglo-French military preparations, halted the supply of U-2 imagery to the British on 30 October 1956.[21]

As operations from Wiesbaden wound down, Adana airfield in Turkey, today known as Incirlik, became the U-2's main European operating base. Turkey was an obvious location from which to launch flights against the southern USSR, but they had to wait until May 1956 for agreement from Prime Minister Menderes. Turkish cooperation was always a delicate subject with its frequently on/off relationship with the Americans. In return for basing, the US was willing to offer some intelligence, mainly related to the neighbouring Syrian air force.[22]

Once aircraft and aircrew arrived 'Det B' became operational at Adana on 11 September. It continued Middle East flights, monitoring Anglo-French preparations against Egypt. Rather than transferring film directly to the US, the Americans made use of USAFE's 497th Reconnaissance Technical Squadron (RTS) at Schierstein, near Wiesbaden, supplemented by personnel from the US to work locally on the U-2 imagery. As there was no processing facility at Adana there was an additional day delay until the film reached Germany. At Adana an improvised processing facility was hastily assembled (URPIC-W, see Chapter 6) to process basic imagery. American flights continued over the zone until halted on 1 February 1957.[23]

Intriguingly, from 6 November 1956 there is a report of NATO air defences being alerted to a high-flying aircraft passing through Turkish airspace, heading towards Egypt. On Cyprus, RAF Hunters were said to have been scrambled and from 50,000ft they positively identified a U-2 flying some several thousand feet above. The CIA record of a mission on that day (1319) remains withheld, although the reason for its retention is unknown.[24]

Beyond Suez and a wider programme of Middle East missions, Det B awaited authorisation for further flights over the USSR. The southern Soviet Union was of great intelligence interest as the location where much nuclear, missile and space programme research and testing was taking place. Soviet air defences along its southern flank were much less dense than in central Europe. Key locations such as Kapustin Yar, Tyuratam and Sary Shagan soon literally became their focal point. Between September 1956 and May 1960, Det B mounted around 168 missions, including approximately 41 primarily ELINT flights. These included 16 over the USSR, 12 of those from Lahore and Peshawar in Pakistan, plus some 152 missions over the Middle East. To that must be added large numbers of training and test flights.

Autumn 1956

Following the Soviet suppression of the Hungarian uprising, on 15 November 1956 Eisenhower grudgingly granted permission for a few missions over Eastern Europe and a shallow penetration flight of the Soviet southern border region. On 20 November Gary Powers flew Mission 4016 about 80nm inside Armenia's and Azerbaijan's borders. A multi-source examination allows the reconstruction of his route. Departing Adana at 0630Z Powers flew through Syria, across to Baghdad and further into Iran, past Dezful and Andimeshk, turning north towards the Caspian Sea. He entered Soviet airspace by Astara Air Base, on the edge of the Caspian, passed over a haze-covered Baku in Soviet Azerbaijan, with the A2 camera imaging Baku-Kala AB, Baku Seaplane base and city as he headed towards the Armenian capital Yerevan. Over Leninakan AB (today Gyumri) Powers' U-2 experienced an electrical inverter fault that caused instrument failure. This, and deteriorating weather, saw him

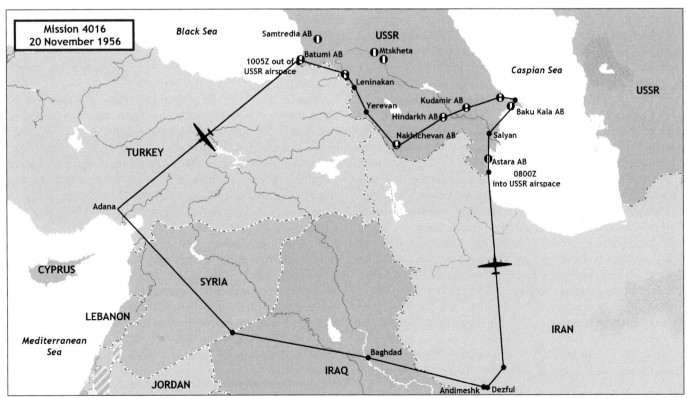

Mission 4016 was a shallow Soviet airspace penetration mission flown by Gary Powers the latter part curtailed by an electrical fault. (Map by Tom Cooper, based on CIA data)

terminate the mission. He had covered most of his assigned targets, though was forced to abandon four others in southern Georgia. Leaving Soviet airspace near Batumi – close to the Georgian–Turkish border – he headed directly to Adana. His System I recorder had failed 25 minutes after take-off, but System III captured several transmissions. From the post-mission analysis Powers was first reported in Soviet airspace as he passed Astara. The tracking of the aircraft was intermittent, he was not always identified as 'hostile' or even 'suspicious' by Soviet air defences and they even lost contact of him for 90 minutes. Some of the mission's most important intelligence included detection of a new airfield constructed near Baku, plus photographing improvements being made to others. The post-flight report observed how differently Soviet air defence operations functioned in Baku compared to Tiblisi.[25]

10 December 1956, saw two flights that covered target areas in Bulgaria, one from Det A's new facilities at Gibelstadt with another from Det B. Mission 2029 saw Carmine Devito leave Gibelstadt at 0749Z and head south. His 6hr 47min flight covered targets in Albania, Bulgaria, Romania and Yugoslavia using the A2. Meanwhile Buster Edens, in Art 350 (4018) departed Adana at 0556Z for his 7hr 19min flight that took in a Yugoslav target and large numbers in Bulgaria with his B camera. Both pilots imaged around the capital Sofia and the airfield at Karlovo. This new series of overflights was short lived. Another presidential order forbade further missions following a mass SAC RB-57D flight over Vladivostock and the Eastern USSR on 18 December that created a voluble Soviet protest.

SIGINT Operations

The development of effective SIGINT collection equipment was often a trial and error process. But gradually data from these flights built-up a picture of Soviet radar and SAM systems' locations and capabilities. Unfortunately, there is very limited publicly available data relating to SIGINT from these missions. Those details that are available are mostly generalised, in summary form. There are occasional COMINT snippets, but no systematic declassification of records.

Following the debacle of the SAC Far East RB-57D mission, U-2 operations were switched to peripheral flights with the first on 22 December 1956 (4019). This carried System V, a SIGINT payload, which left no room for the main camera. Pilot Tom Birkhead flew along the Soviet border from the Black Sea, past the Caspian Sea on to Afghanistan, collecting Soviet air defence transmissions. His flight became rather complex. As the weather turned to a complete undercast, he had to rely on compass and sextant for navigation. Unfortunately, his compass had a significant error so he was forced to 'play safe' and fly further from Soviet border areas than originally intended. His System V and other electrical equipment was affected by a generator failure after six hours, but the recorders had used all their tape. One of the three receivers failed too, about one to two hours in the mission. Following analysis of the ELINT material a lack of detected signals was determined to be because there were none, rather than due to equipment failures.[26] This was another indicator that Soviet radar coverage along its southern border was sporadic.

Mission 2037 was an early ELINT flight on 11 October 1957. Over the very sensitive Barents Sea it was the penultimate operational mission for Det A at Giebelstadt before its closure. Planned to monitor Soviet naval exercises, piloted by Jacob Kratt in Art 351, it was the first operational use of the new 'System IV' equipment.[27] Ramo-Wooldridge manufactured this 'ferret' system that used frequency sweeping receivers, a 14 channel magnetic tape recorder, oscilloscope and film recorder.[28] A later, July 1958 document, shows

it was rushed into service for these two ELINT missions (2037 and 2040), covering the Barents and Baltic Sea, a priority ARC target.[29] As Kratt approached Tromsø in northern Norway he turned on 'System IV' and began collecting transmissions for three and a half hours. For the majority of his flight, he could not see the ground due to the undercast, with navigation done by dead reckoning. It was only as he exited the area that he managed to see the Norwegian coast and calculated that he was 54 miles south of his intended position. He finally landed in Germany after nearly 10 hours and having flown 3,900 nautical miles.[30]

As mentioned in Chapter 1, the use of System IV was not a smooth process nor was it really effective. There was significant electronic interference to the equipment from the aircraft itself. Following the difficulties experienced in 1957 there was a programme to speedily correct the deficiencies of the seven sets the CIA had purchased.[31] In further flights: Mission 4078 on 15 March 1958 experienced a serious System IV failure. Nothing significant is known about Mission 4079 along the Soviet border on 7 May 1958. The newly modified System IV sets were put into the field for further test flights from 3 to 24 June 1958 flown from Adana. The four known missions (102, 103, 104, 105) were effectively 'operational tests' of the modified System IV flown over the Black Sea, Turkey and Iran along the southern Soviet border using Articles 351 and 352.

After that System IV was only used on a few further occasions. First, for the 'Big Ears' missions over the US 6th Fleet to record its electronic transmissions as it operated in the Mediterranean on 11 August 1958. The second, Mission 4096 on 4 December 1958, was used to monitor the launch of the Soviet space rocket Luna which exploded 245 seconds after launch from Baikonour. Third, on 2 January 1959, a mission along the Soviet/Afghanistan border, successfully captured the launch of Soviet lunar probe 'Metchta'.[32] Further tests in August 1959 indicated that removing the all-important tracker camera significantly improved System IV's performance.[33] Finally it was used for the diversionary missions (8007 and 8010) in December 1959 and February 1960 to support the RAF's two deep Soviet penetration flights. In April 1960 the ARC recommended System IV's retirement and the equipment was placed into storage.[34]

1957 Highpoint of Soviet Overflights

Eisenhower remained wary of deep penetration missions over the USSR but he eventually relented and authorised further flights. One major priority for US intelligence was to discover the impact location for expected Soviet missile test launches from Kapustin Yar, Tyuratam and Saryshagan. Klyuchi, on the north-east corner of the Kamchatka peninsula in remote Siberia, was prioritised as a U-2 target by the ARC on 13 May 1957, although then uncertain about its possible use. The suspected area was allocated to Eielson's newly activated 'Det C'. The first mission, flown by pilot Al Rand on 8 June 1957 (6002), was abandoned when a continuous undercast made photography impossible. Interestingly though, the mission record shows it was supported by an RB-47 flight that orbited just over 100 miles off the coast with an SA-16 Albatross providing SAR cover. On 20 June Rand re-flew the mission (now 6005) with more success. He photographed some small settlements, plus detected some ongoing construction work and seven Mi-4 'Hound' helicopters at Klyuchi. The missions appeared to have attracted no Russian attention.[35]

Project RAINBOW

Well aware that the window of opportunity was closing on the U-2 and as a direct response to the detection of the initial flights over

Europe during 1956, serious efforts began to make them radar 'invisible.' Sometimes referred to as 'anti-radar technology,' better understood today as 'stealth,' the Agency attempted to reduce the U-2's vulnerability. Named project 'RAINBOW' it involved staff from Lockheed and Westinghouse with more than $353,000 allocated for research in 1957 and 1958.[36] The modified aircraft became known to pilots and crews as 'Dirty Birds.'

One form of modification, described as a 'Trapeze,' involved fitting short fibreglass poles along the U-2's wings, fuselage and tail with small gauge wire strung between them. The idea, stemmed, at least in part, from a phenomenon observed when missiles were fired. An 'ionised layer' was created by the missiles' exhaust heat from the launch that reduced its radar reflectivity. It was suggested that application of a power source around the skin of the U-2 would have a similar effect.[37] It was hoped that the wires would absorb, or at least weaken, Soviet radar signals, to prevent a readable return to the ground operators.

The other approach involved fixing a circuit board-like material to the U-2's flat surfaces to absorb pulses from Soviet 65-85 Megahertz frequency range radars. It was of no use against radars operating outside those frequencies. Known as 'wallpaper', it caused airframe heat retention resulting in

Art 349 'Dirty Bird' was fitted with a 'trapeze' of fibreglass poles with thin wires run between them attempting to reduce its radar return. (CIA)

Work on preparing the surface of Art 341, the other 'Dirty Bird' prior to application of an early form of radar absorbent material. (CIA)

engine over-heating and flameouts. It resulted in one crash, killing test pilot Robert Sieker, on 4 April 1957 in Art 341, the very first U-2 built. Both designs also had 'radar absorbent material' treatments applied.[38]

The system was to be tested operationally with two Dirty Birds sent to both Det B and Det C. Jim Cherbonneaux with Det B, flew the first of two missions on 21 July 1957 (4030) in Art 344. He was not best pleased with the Dirty Bird. As he described: 'I had never risked flying an airplane wired like a guitar.' The modifications significantly reduced the aircraft's operational ceiling and range.[39]

Photography from Mission 4030 covered Kirkuk in Iraq, part of Iran and along the Azeri coast close to Baku again. He flew a second mission on 31 July (4033) described as an 'ELINT and coastal reconnaissance mission', he flew a clockwise course overwater

close to Bulgarian and Crimean coasts entering the Aegean before returning to Adana. The priority for both pilots was not imagery but carrying System V to eavesdrop on Soviet air defence transmissions as the Dirty Bird flew by.[40] As Cherbonneaux explained: 'The plan was to see if the Soviets could detect our Dirty Bird. All in all, the coatings and wire worked well, but analysis of the recordings indicated that the bad guys were homing in on my cockpit and tailpipe, neither of which had been treated.'[41]

Even as the first operational sorties were being flown, internal memos expressed that the RAINBOW programme: 'Had experienced only a measured success.'[42] However, despite the RAINBOW programmes' problems, a Dirty Bird took part in possibly the U-2's most successful series of Soviet overflights in the summer of 1957.

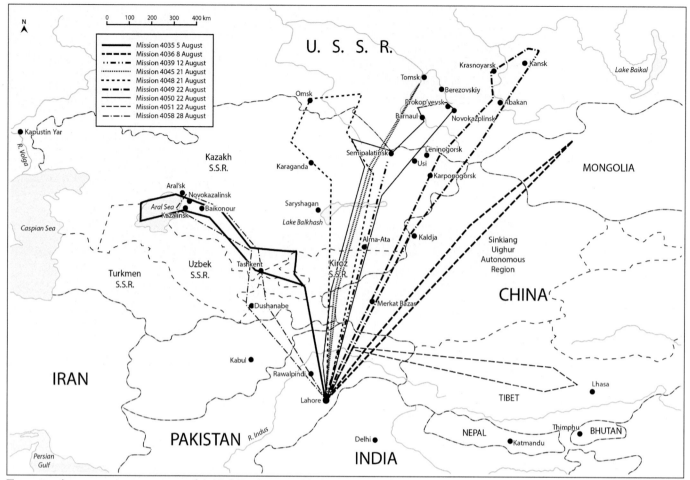

The routes show approximate coverage of the Soft Touch series of flights emanating from Lahore in Pakistan. This was the largest series of Soviet overflights and stimulated rapid construction of Soviet air defences in the southern republics. (Map by George Anderson, adapted from CIA map, Pedlow and Welzenbach p.145).

Soft Touch

During August 1957 nine missions were launched from Lahore in Pakistan. The advanced party for this Soft Touch series of flights arrived from Adana in mid-July together with three aircraft: Art 353, 356 and 'Dirty Bird' Art 344. These were very deep penetration flights that used a mix of A and B camera configurations. Most headed to an arc of targets than spanned from Lahore to the Aral Sea as its most westerly point, to Mongolia in the east.

The combined mission results were described as 'sensational' by the CIA's Photo Interpreters. They produced: 'A veritable bonanza of scientific and technical information that kept scores of PIs and other analysts in the intelligence community busy for more than a year.'[43] Their first mission, on August 4 (4036), penetrated to an area to the southwest of Irkutsk close to the Russian-Mongolian border. Its System I picked up no VHF communications and neither did its S-band ELINT set. On the return from that mission Gary Powers had to make a dead-stick landing back at Lahore after a flameout on his return leg in Art 353.[44] The following day, 4035 covered the Aral Sea area using the Dirty Bird aircraft with further flights by Art 344 for missions: 4039, 4048, 4050 and 4058. Mission 4045 reached to Lake Issyk Kul in the Kyrgyz Republic and the Xinjiang region of north-west China. It also imaged the important nuclear facilities, then in their early stages, in the 'nuclear city' of Tomsk.

Vozrozhdeniya Island

Soft Touch Mission 4035 on 5 August 1957 likely provided the first overflight imagery of Vozrozhdeniya Island in the inland Aral Sea. Declassified CIA documents usually ensure mentions of nuclear, biological and chemical programmes and related installations remain redacted and, indeed, this is the case for Vozrozhdeniya Island. However, a small part of the analysis from Mission 4035 has escaped the censors' grasp. Using its B camera, some 134 images appear to have covered the site. That imagery identified a wide range of docks, barracks, storage areas, warehouse buildings, communications facilities 'test sites' and somewhat ominously 'burial grounds', presumably for dead animals. Using the images, a large number of scale and oblique drawings were prepared to illustrate the facilities to senior analysis and policy makers.[45] Vozrozhdeniya was an explicit target for the next U-2 flight over the region on 9 July 1959 when Mission 4125 (Touchdown) targeted the Aral Sea on its exit route to Zahedan in Iran.

Nuclear Testing Ground

Approaching midnight on 21 August 1957, Lahore airfield must have been a hive of activity. Three U-2s departed within the space of just 45 minutes all on different routes. Tom Birkhead left in Art 353 for Mission 4049. This covered the central Asiatic region of the USSR reaching as far north as Maksikha close to the Kazakh, Russian, Chinese border but was adversely affected by cloud.

For Mission 4050 Jim Cherbonneaux was again the pilot in Dirty Bird Art 344. Limited to a maximum 58,500ft altitude because of the extra weight of the 'anti-radar' equipment, his flight lasted 8hrs 15min. He photographed what soon became another high priority target, the Saryshagan radar test site, close to Lake Balkash, plus Omsk and Semipalatinsk.[47]

CLOSED TOMSK

An early coup was the imaging of the nuclear facilities around Tomsk (renamed Seversk). Tomsk was a closed city until 1992; it housed two early nuclear reactors, spent fuel processing, uranium enrichment plant and other related facilities.

This image from Mission 4045 shows the Tomsk site very much in its early construction phase. The original reactor building is on the centre left with the long buildings being part of the early processing complex and the start of six circular cooling towers. (NARA)

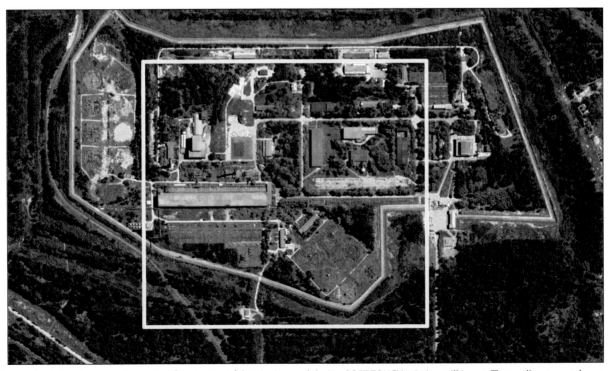

This recent satellite imagery shows significant parts of the site imaged during SOFT TOUCH mission still intact. The cooling towers have gone as have many of the early buildings. The city remains important to Russian nuclear activities. (Maxar)

VOZROZHDENIYA BIOLOGICAL WEAPONS PROVING GROUND

Knowledge of this site only became more widely known in the west after the end of the Cold War. Small numbers of unexplained deaths in the area have been reported over the years, suggesting accidental exposures. In 1971, a scientist on the research vessel *Lev Berg*, contracted smallpox after it passed through a 'brownish haze,' a cloud of 'weaponized' smallpox. She recovered but went on to infect nine other people, three of whom died, including her

brother, after she returned home. The incident was suppressed by the Soviet government. In 1979 there was an escape of anthrax near Sverdlovsk. As a result, the Soviet government decided to dispose of its stockpile and transported 100-200 tonnes of 'anthrax slurry' to pits on Vozrozhdeniya in 1988. The facility was abandoned in the 1990s.[46]

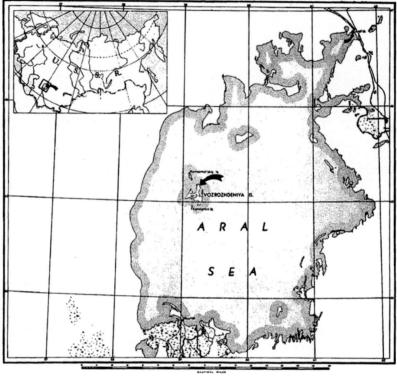

Vozrozhdeniya Island was located in the middle of the inland Aral Sea in Uzbekistan. Surrounded by water it was considered ideal as a chemical/biological test site. (CIA)

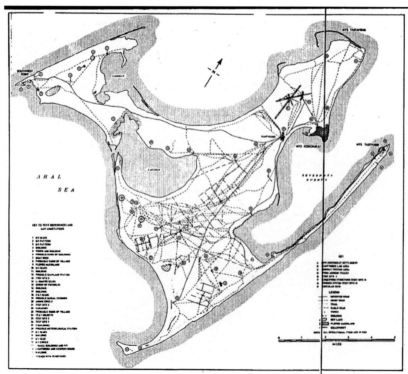

Drawings prepared from imagery shows tracks and main features of the island. (CIA)

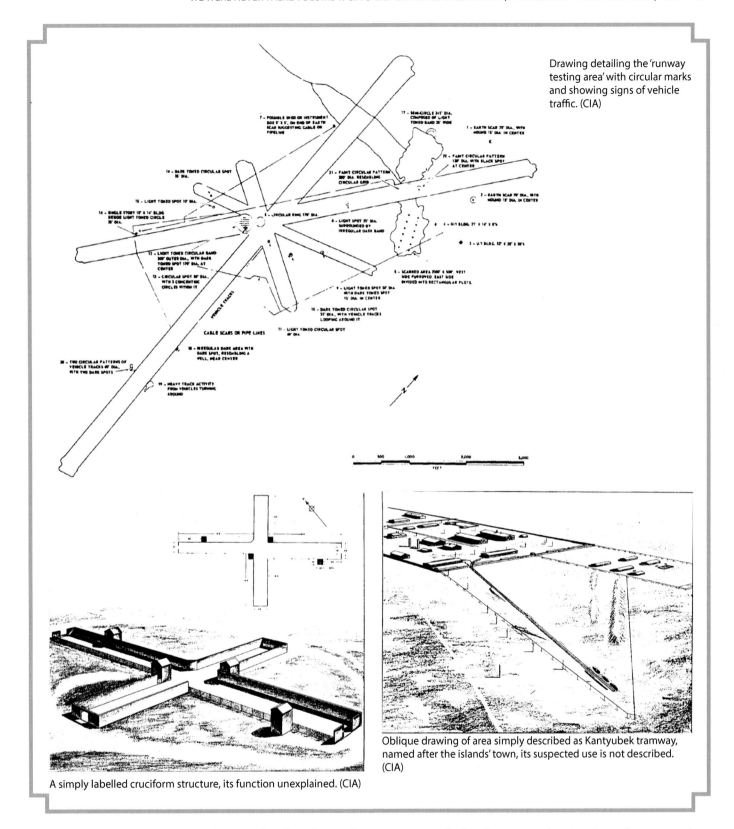

Drawing detailing the 'runway testing area' with circular marks and showing signs of vehicle traffic. (CIA)

A simply labelled cruciform structure, its function unexplained. (CIA)

Oblique drawing of area simply described as Kantyubek tramway, named after the islands' town, its suspected use is not described. (CIA)

Henry S. Lowenhaupt, was an analyst in CIA's Office of Scientific Intelligence. In July 1957 he was asked to work up target briefs for all potential atomic sites within Soviet Central Asia and Siberia. As he said the Americans knew that:

Twenty-odd nuclear tests had occurred near there in the last eight years, but the exact location of any test was not known closer than within thirty miles. I had no idea how big the test area was… As [a mission] targeter, I became involved in selecting the flight path because the best photography, that from the vertical angle, covered a band only five miles wide.

To try and identify a precise location Lowenhaupt turned to Dr Donald Rock from the US Air Force Technical Applications Center and asked him to average the seismic epicentres of the five largest previous nuclear detonations in the region to produce a 'centroid' point. That analysis derived a spot in the desert around 70 miles west of Semipalatinsk, a place with no name, passed only by the odd desert caravan on a trail close to some seasonally dry salt lakes. Cherbonneaux's flight brought an unexpected sighting at Semipalatinsk; seeing a tower in the desert, it reminded him of the Yucca Flats nuclear test site in the US. He flicked the camera switch on and began imaging the site. After landing back at Lahore he was lampooned for his debrief that reported Semipalatinsk as a possible nuclear testing ground. Within 24 hours, a nuclear explosion took place there and the developed images from his overflight proved his observation, taken just a few hours before its detonation.[48]

Lownhaupt explained in a later interview that:

It was actually four hours later that 'Joe 36' was detonated; it was airdropped and went half a megaton. The pilot had photographed it and its carrier aircraft on the ground when he had flown over the Semipalatinsk airfield and associated nuclear weapon assembly facility. The nuclear weapon 'cab' he apprehensively spotted on the shot-tower at the proving ground was for a low-yield device that was not to be detonated until 13 September.[49]

His left oblique camera failed after just 104 frames on the flight. Though heavily redacted, the post-mission report shows Jim Charbonneaux imaged 360 square miles of the nuclear site and identified: 'at least eight ground zeros, shot tower and instrumentation, auxiliary airfield and limited support facilities.'[50]

Amongst all this detail, it is sometimes difficult to remember that U-2 pilots like Jim Charbonneaux have seen the Earth as few of us ever will. He described on his return leg to Lahore 'I saw the shimmering snowy peak of the awesome mountain called K2 illuminated against a dark blue sky. K2 was my beacon back to Pakistan.' The remaining mission, 4051, was flown by Bill Hall in Art 356. He headed east as far as Lhasa in Tibet but found 'no targets of immediate intelligence interest', the only significant urban settlement being Lhasa.

The major achievements of the Soft Touch series were considerable, including the first imaging of Tyuratam launch site, identifying Saryshagan and the Semipalatinsk nuclear testing

ground. These arguably made this the most successful series of Soviet U-2 photographic overflights.

Dirty Birds Again

On their return from Lahore, Det B used its Dirty Birds just three more times operationally. Mission 4059 was a deep penetration mission over the southern USSR on 10 September 1957. Bill Hall photographed a large number of airfields and importantly provided extensive high-quality imagery of the Kapustin Yar missile range. The site was at the top of the target priority list. The final two Dirty Bird flights were ELINT missions over the Black Sea (4061 on 27 September and 4067 on 21 November). Their equipment included System I and III and appear mainly aimed at gauging how effectively Arts. 344 and 349 could be detected and tracked by the Soviets similar to Cherbonneaux's July flight. They flew the same overwater route as Mission 4033 had on 31 July 1957.

Det C used its two allocated 'Dirty Birds' (Art 355 and 378) for just one mission each. 6008 on September 16 flown by Baker from Eielson in Art 355. Again, the target was the Kamchatka peninsula, to detect construction or activity at Klychi. By 25 October 1957 Art 355 had been returned to Edwards AFB. Art 378 flew its only Det C mission (6011) from Astugi on 1 March 1958.[51] This was a very successful overflight that captured a large number of important targets for the first time around Komsomolsk and the strategic bomber airfield at Ukraina.[52] This single overflight provoked a strong Soviet protest that persuaded Eisenhower to put a brake on further missions again. Eisenhower seemed concerned that more overflights might provide a superficial justification for Khrushchev to move on Berlin, where tensions were high again.[53]

Project RAINBOW was discontinued as largely unsuccessful and had significantly degraded the U-2's performance. The

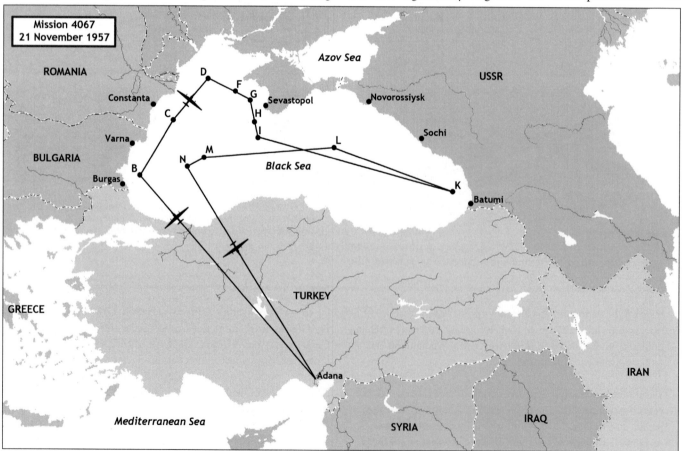

4067 was a final Dirty Bird mission over the Black Sea to collect data on Soviet air defence radar reactions to the flight. (Map by Tom Cooper, based on CIA data)

The U-2's wings were only secured by a few bolts, and a number of other control and fuel connections. This is the Smithsonian's U-2 prior to its reassembly and display and makes it easy to understand why many worried about its fragility. (NASM)

aircraft were soon de-modified. Art 367 was retained at Edwards AFB for installation and testing the new 'C' camera.[54] Art 344 was reconfigured as the platform for System VII to be used for Soviet ballistic missile launch missions with Det B. Art 349 was 'deconverted' from its Dirty Bird configuration at Burbank in June-July 1958 and remained at Edwards.[55]

That U-2s were so frequently upgraded and modified for special one-off tasks pays great tribute to the robustness and flexibility of such a seemingly delicate basic design. For many aircraft types making the major modifications required for the RAINBOW aircraft, or radically redesigning sensor fits, would have seen the reworked airframes having to be discarded afterwards. Not so the U-2, change the wings, the aft fuselage, rework the equipment bay and it was good to go again. An astounding achievement.

Increasing Threat

Long gone were any hopes that the U-2 could operate undetected and untracked. Constantly on the CIA's collective mind was the question of just how long they could continue to overfly the Soviet Union. The Agency regularly reviewed the threats facing the aircraft. In February 1957 CIA Assistant Director Herbet Scoville reassessed Soviet height finding radar performance to reflect their capabilities to accurately identify the U-2's operating altitudes. However, the capability for Soviet fighter aircraft to reach those altitudes was still assessed as 'low.'[56] Air defences were described as being most capable around Moscow, Leningrad and Kapustin Yar. By 1959

forecasts suggested that Soviet air defences would soon be able to shoot down a U-2 as their Surface to Air Missile (SAM) capability was rapidly improving.

Scoville's memo outlined the geographical coverage and capabilities of Soviet air defence radars at that time. It indicated an almost total certainty of detection and tracking:

- Everywhere in the USSR and European satellites west of the Urals and the Caspian
- Almost certain detection and tracking in the Soviet Far East and eastern China
- Almost certain detection in the northern USSR except between Novya Zemlya and Wrangel Island where 'detection is uncertain,' but high probability around Tiksi
- Complete detection along southern borders east of Caspian to Tashkent. But from Tashkent to Chita a low probability of detection

Close to the Aral Sea, and east of the Urals to the Arctic 'coastal strip' were still believed to be largely devoid of significant military infrastructure, including radar. The threat to the U-2's safety was constantly evolving but the intelligence they produced was unrivalled. The CIA's Richard Bissell much later recalled that by 1959 U-2 missions were providing '90 percent of our hard intelligence information about the Soviet Union.'[57]

3
OLDSTER

Although known through authors like Chris Pocock and Paul Lashman, for many years the UK government consistently refused to publicly admit any significant British involvement with the U-2 programme. Such connections long remained a very sensitive topic, with only a slow drip of information seeping out. In January 2019, a small number of key detailed files were finally released to the UK National Archive.[1]

The story of British U-2 operations is as much a political as a military one. After Prime Minister Anthony Eden was swept aside following the Suez debacle, Harold Macmillan's premiership was a recovery period for intelligence operations.[2] Anglo-American relations were rapidly restored with senior British government members, including Macmillan, regularly briefed on U-2 operations again. Details and copy images were briefed to an RAF Air Commodore (and his assistant) based in Washington DC, then brought to Britain and shown to the Prime Minister, a few senior military officers, ministers and officials.[3] Perhaps following the

precedent established by the 'Jiu Jitsu' missions in 1952 and 1954, the US became interested in British involvement with the U-2 programme.

Various explanations have been advanced for British involvement in U-2 operations. One, purportedly from CIA Director Allen Dulles, suggested that if the British undertook missions during sensitive US electoral periods, this would keep the U-2s operating more or less continuously.[4] From a British perspective participation has been described as a means to justify continued access to the 'take' from US operations, or simply as part of the 'US-UK special relationship.' The explanation is probably different from both sides, certainly multifaceted. Participation was not solely an act of US altruism, nor British practicality. It was, for a period at least, regarded as of high value, mutual self-interest.

British interest accelerated during 1957. Macmillan agreed that four RAF pilots would be trained to fly the U-2. Flt Lts John MacArthur, David Dowling, Michael Bradley and Squadron Leader Chris Walker were all sent to Laughlin AFB, Del Rio, Texas for training. Tragedy struck almost immediately when Chris Walker died on 8 July 1958. Departing for a high altitude training flight in Art 380 he suffered hypoxia, due to a build-up of ice in the oxygen system, and consequently lost control of his aircraft. Unsuccessfully attempting to escape, he crashed near Amarillo over 450 miles from Del Rio. He was replaced by newly promoted Squadron Leader Robert 'Robbie' Robinson.

Robinson, on a return flight to the UK after completing high altitude nuclear fallout sampling missions over the Christmas Island test site, in a Canberra, was summoned to the Air Ministry.

> Clearly they were looking for someone to quickly replace Chris Walker. I was told to report to the Assistant Chief of the Air Staff, AVM John Grandy in London. He asked me "Can you go to America tomorrow? I can't tell you what it is about, but it involves flying at high altitude and then working somewhere in Europe." So, I said yes.[5]

The first three pilots joined Det B at Adana during November 1958, Robinson arrived soon after.

In Downing Street and Whitehall the fear of political fallout from any potential British overflight incident was considerable. Macmillan placed a number of conditions on UK participation. 'British' missions were to be flown by 'civil' pilots (not RAF). The aircraft were not to wear RAF markings and operational flights required specific Prime Ministerial approval.[6] In December 1958 a final exchange of letters confirmed the operational arrangements in which Macmillan reserved the right to be the final approving authority for all flights using British pilots.

OLDSTER

The operational plan, signed between the RAF and CIA on 28 October 1958, was a project named 'OLDSTER.' MI6 assisted the Air Ministry with clandestine elements of the operation. Overall command was vested with distinguished wartime bomber pilot Group Captain Thomas Bingham-Hall DSO, DFC on 12 November 1958. His cover was as 'CO Meteorological Experimental Research

Newly promoted Squadron Leader 'Robbie' Robinson was the British element CO of Det B at Adana. (Via Paul Lashman)

Unit' (MEU), to be based at RAF Watton, Norfolk. He also maintained an office at the Air Ministry in London and was responsible to the Assistant Chief of Air Staff (Operations). Individual British flights were controlled via the 'Air Ministry Operations Centre,' later named the 'Air Force Operations Centre,' with links to the Cabinet Office and Defence Operations Centre. Most communications on U-2 related work were handled via the CIA/USAF HBJAYWALK communications network, which sometimes activated a temporary node at Watton.

An exchange of notes and letters between Macmillan and Eisenhower gives a detailed picture of how the British U-2 use would dovetail into CIA operations. In a memo to Eisenhower, via the British Ambassador on 11 December 1958, Macmillan says:

> The staffs on both sides have now worked out an agreed procedure for clearance and I have now approved in principle a programme of British flights for the next three months, of which details will be available to you. I have ruled that within this programme each individual flight should be submitted to me for clearance before it is made…

Eisenhower's response specified:

> I think it should be understood, however, that British missions are carried out on your authority and are your responsibility just as our activities are authorized and controlled here in accordance with procedures I have established. In this sense, it could be said that we are carrying out two complementary programmes rather than a joint one.

The Director of Central Intelligence, Allen Dulles insisted that title to the aircraft used by the British operationally must rest with them.[7]

For UK flights the British sought broad US assent then planned missions in detail through the normal U-2 CHALICE process. At that stage the US could veto individual British proposals.[8] The UK Joint Intelligence Committees' initial priority was identification of Soviet nuclear bomber bases that could be used to attack Britain. The US focus was already shifting towards Soviet missile development and deployment. Therefore, to secure US agreement British priorities had to be balanced with American ones. British approval for sorties reached Macmillan having been passed up, via the Foreign Office Permanent Under Secretary, the Vice Chief of the Air Staff, Secretary of State for Air, and the Foreign Secretary for 'provisional political clearance.' When secured, it was notified to US authorities.[9]

Final approval to launch the mission was passed by signal to the RAF Liaison Officer at Adana no less than five hours before the scheduled departure.[10] Whilst the British planning process was parallel to the American one it was certainly not independent of it. This approach ensured that the British could fly missions, but not spring any surprises on the Americans.

Much later, the British approval process, said to have worked reasonably well by CIA's Acting Assistant Director for Special Activities also found the 'British system of approvals a bit tedious, since no less than eight senior Air Ministry and government officials, including the Prime Minister had to sign off on each mission and any other minor changes to the flight plan.'[11] It certainly made any last-minute mission-plan changes frustrating for all concerned.

British Cover Story

The OLDSTER unit devised various cover stories in case a British U-2 mission was lost. It was considered vital to protect American U-2 operations and their use of Adana. The British pilots were to be nominally civilian, employed by the Meteorological Office, rather the Royal Air Force. If a British pilot was lost in an incident it was to be claimed that the aircraft had been conducting a weather flight from Peshawar, headed to a 'British base on Cyprus.' The use of Adana, in any event, to be explained by the better maintenance facilities there than were available on Cyprus. If a British pilot was ever captured by the Russians, they were simply instructed to tell the truth on the basis that: 'The Russians would get the story out of the pilot anyway and if he told the truth at once it could save him from the worst treatment.'[12] Meanwhile the British authorities intended to simply try and cast doubt on the accuracy of any Soviet protests.

Meteorological Flights

A memo from Richard Bissell outlined to Eisenhower's Chief of Staff, General Andrew Goodpaster at the White House of British preparations U-2 operations. It also told the President that two U-2s were soon to be staged through RAF Watton to fly a small number of 'meteorological missions.'[13] The CIA had agreed to make a U-2 available for the British to fulfil their wish: 'to conduct a minimum of two successful meteorological research missions from Watton

Fictitious serials were part of U-2 life. Here, marked '417,' Art 349 sits at RAF Watton in May 1959 ready to fly two RAF meteorological missions as part of its cover and as a discreet test of the 'Fast Move' staging concept. (TNA, via Chris Pocock)

1959 U-2 RAF METEOROLOGICAL FLIGHTS

Four operational weather flights were mounted from the HQ of the specially formed RAF Meteorological Experimental Research Unit at RAF Watton during 1959. Each flight adopted a slightly different route, but their main purpose was to help cement cover for British involvement in U-2 operations. The flights tested the 'Fast Move' concept again.

This USAF C-54 was used by the CIA to move the advance party to RAF Watton on 3 October 1959. It was photographed later at Dublin Airport. (Paul Howard via Mick West)

322nd Air Division C-130s provided the heavy lift element for 'Fast Move' staging operations. (USAF)

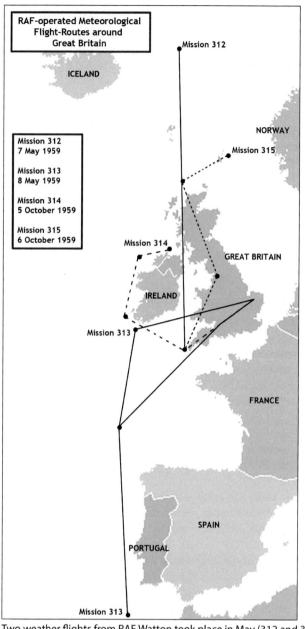

RAF-operated Meteorological Flight-Routes around Great Britain

Mission 312
7 May 1959

Mission 313
8 May 1959

Mission 314
5 October 1959

Mission 315
6 October 1959

Two weather flights from RAF Watton took place in May (312 and 313), with two more in October 1959 (314 and 315). It was only on the latter two flights that the full Weather Packages were carried. (Map by Tom Cooper, based on CIA data)

to further British cover story and provide British Meteorological Office with upper air data.' RAF Kinloss was to be made available as a staging field to support operational missions if required.[14]

At RAF Watton secure space was cleared in Hangar 2 for two U-2s that would 'belong' to the MEU for its tasks. The Commandant of Watton's Central Signals Establishment was briefed on their real role. He was also responsible for the peripheral SIGINT collection missions flown by the stations 51 Squadron Comets and Canberras.[15] The 'OLDSTER' unit at the Air Ministry controlled all MEU activities and support.[16] Watton was additionally to handle CIA U-2s being ferried between Adana and the US, to further strengthen the MEU cover story.

The first weather flights were scheduled from 10 December 1958 onwards. Although the aircraft and support arrived at Watton, the missions were abandoned, ironically due to near continuous heavy

fog, difficult for the U-2s to handle. For its return to Adana 'radar suppression' was practised as it transited through Mildenhall, Manston, Lyon, Pisa, Taranto, Araxos and Athens control zones. Radar suppression could take different forms. The various radar units were pre-warned that an aircraft would pass through its coverage. They simply ignored the contact, maintaining only a listening watch as it followed a specified route, or passed through at a notified time, normally high above any other traffic. Air traffic ensured that any calls from the U-2 were answered with no information that might give away its position, altitude, bearing or course.[17] The aircraft returned to Adana on 21 December 1958 using the anodyne callsign 'Air Force Jet 9304,' ready for the first British Middle East overflight on 31 December 1958.[18]

Art 349 is now proudly displayed in the USAF Museum of Aviation at Warner Robins AFB. (Museum of Aviation)

hydraulic leak and fuel counter failure forced the flight to be abandoned and an emergency diversion to RAF Brize Norton. A repair party was quickly despatched by RAF aircraft. They carried out a temporary repair that enabled the U-2 to return to Watton. The deployment passed U-2 Art 351 through Watton on its ferry flight back to Edwards AFB and moved Art 344, now equipped with System VII equipment, in the opposite direction.[24]

This process was repeated on 5 and 6 October 1959 (Missions 314 and 315). CIA 'after action' reports give a detailed account of that second deployment as another Fast Move test. On 3 October C-54D (42-72627)

Fast Move Concept

'Fast Move' was developed by USAF Colonel Stanley Beerli during 1958 whilst attached to the CIA. It was intended to allow: 'deployment of a self-supporting task force of approximately 30 men and one U-2 aircraft to a remote base' utilising a C-124 and C-130 as support aircraft.[19] It minimised the time U-2s spent on the ground at sensitive third country airfields in Pakistan, Norway, Iran and elsewhere. These forward based operations brought much more Soviet territory within U-2 range and made it more difficult for them to coordinate their air defence responses.[20]

On 7 and 8 May 1959 RAF Watton hosted two successful weather flights. For the CIA the main purpose of this short deployment to England was to test the Fast Move concept, a rehearsal for real operations. At 1815Z on 6 May, C-130A (55-0026) arrived from Adana. The Fast Move operations plan spelt out in great detail the equipment and personnel required for staging operations. Arrangements covered everything from fuel and medical supplies, sleeping bags and rations to water. It included spare fuses, hoists, circuit breakers, clothing, down to two cans of beer and Coca-Cola for the pilots on completion of missions! It amounted to over 20,000lb of cargo and up to 30 personnel.[21]

The C-130A parked on a remote part of the airfield, within 300 yards of the runway. A tent-like 'portable hangar' was erected to cover the U-2's cockpit.[22] Operating under their public cover of 'Weather Reconnaissance Squadron Provisional Two' (WRSP-2) U-2 Art 349 flew weather missions (312 and 313) on successive days. The specialist Weather Package (WP) consisted of: 'Instrumentation to measure and record airspeed, altitude, free air temperature, humidity, acceleration, time and aircraft heading,' plus a tracker camera. Weather Package 2 (WP-2) did not operate properly because the RADAN equipment, necessary to make it fully functional, was yet to be installed.[23] Mission 312 routed direct to Lands End and then headed north following the six degrees west meridian up past the north coast of Scotland before reversing course and heading back to Watton.

Mission 313 was flown from Watton to a point off the southern coast of Ireland before it turned south following the 10 degrees west meridian, similar to the previous day's flight. Paralleling the Portuguese coast, at some point he reversed course. Headed north, a

landed at 0900Z to deliver an advance personnel party to Watton, followed by a 322 Air Division C-130A (56-0532) the next day. This time greater use was made of improved facilities that had been set aside in Hangar 2 for MEU U-2 operations. There more electrical points, heating and secure rooms had been prepared since the previous May, with personnel accommodated in officers' and sergeants' messes.[25]

Art 349 was again used for the deployment. It left Adana (ferry flight BF 59-11) at 0100Z on 5 October. There were radio transmission problems in notifying the staging party of its departure, whilst at Watton, there were worries that incoming weather might pose landing problems for it. Diversion arrangements were put in hand but 349 safely landed at Watton at 0630Z. It was immediately prepared for its first mission. The portable hangar was erected around the cockpit. Parked closer to the control tower and hangars this time. Art 349 was positioned just behind the C-130A. Fuel was transferred from 50-gallon drums, using hand pumps and the U-2 made ready. Forty-five minutes before departure it was towed to the engine start-up position close to the active runway.

The pilot had pre-breathed oxygen in the back of the C-130. Just before his departure, a small leak was noted in his helmet faceplate. To maintain the pilot's pre-breathing effort, he held his breath whilst a technician quickly took off the helmet. The pilot briefly used a standard portable A–13 oxygen mask, whilst the technician prepared, then refitted his helmet with a spare faceplate brought on board the C-130. He snapped down the faceplate and quickly resealed the pilot's pressure suit. Taking off less than four hours after landing, at 1015Z, the flight was just 15 minutes late. Mission 314 lasted 6hrs 10mins. It followed a clockwise course out from Lands End out around the west coast of Ireland. Preparations for Mission 315 were moved into hangar two, guarded at night by RAF Police with dog patrols. The second mission was flown the following day, launched at 0900Z and lasted 6hrs 30mins. From Lands End it flew over central England and Scotland to a point east of the Shetlands before heading directly back to Watton. Now with the PC-211 RADAN instrumentation installed, WP-2 was said to have performed well although DC power was lost about two-thirds of the way through the mission. Both flights used tracker cameras using 650ft and 635ft of film respectively. Both also used their System III recorders. After landing Art 349 quickly turned around and departed for Adana at 1740Z on 6 October as BF 59-12. It arrived back in Turkey at 2245Z. The C-130 staging party was due to depart at 0300Z on 7 October 1959, but an aircraft fault delayed that for 24 hours. Despite this last hiccup, it proved a useful test of the staging concept. Whilst these flights fulfilled a useful function, real attention was turning to preparations for operational deep penetration missions.

4
MIDDLE EAST OVERFLIGHTS

U-2 photographic flights of the Middle East began with Det A in August 1956. These were largely around the Mediterranean rim aimed at quantifying Anglo-French preparations for the Suez invasion. Once Det B was established at Adana mission numbers greatly increased and coverage extended from Egypt, Saudi Arabia, Iraq, Iran as far as Kuwait. Between 1956–60 this amounted to approximately 152 – primarily photographic – missions.

Why were there so many? First, the various Middle East tensions and military conflicts along Israel's borders, were of importance to the Americans. Whilst the British colonial presence in the region was rapidly contracting, its interests remained substantial. Soviet military supplies to the region (especially to Egypt and Syria) were also of interest. Political instabilities in Lebanon, Jordan, Iraq, Iran and elsewhere all triggered reconnaissance flights too.

These missions had major training value for pilots waiting to resume Soviet overflights. Middle East missions were unlikely to be intercepted. As Robbie Robinson explained, 'Our bread and butter work was over the Middle East. These were our most productive [missions] because the weather was generally so good … we knew where everyone was – including the Israelis. They were the only people who cottoned on and realized our aeroplanes were overflying them, which they were not happy about.'[1] He suggested that Syrian air defence radars sometimes detected the U-2s as they departed and returned to Adana.

The lack of detection meant pilots could concentrate on becoming proficient at handling the U-2, navigation, turning cameras and equipment on and off, largely free of severe danger from opposition fighters and missiles. When the British element of Det B became active, policy dictated that before the pilots could be considered for Soviet overflights they had to complete at least two Middle East missions.[2]

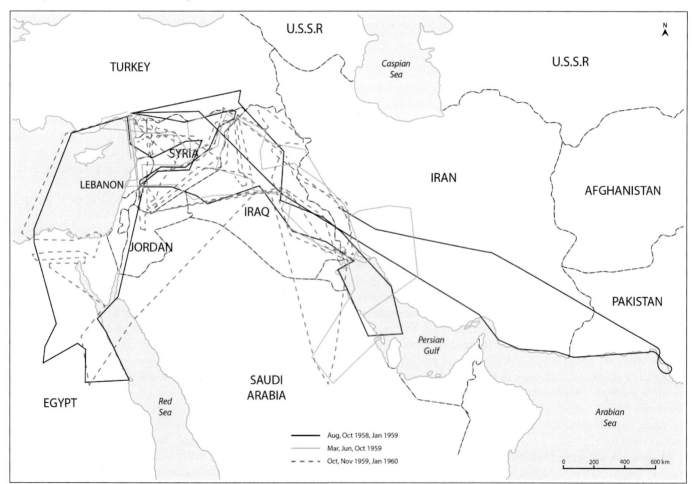

Map shows the extent of overlap of 11 declassified mission routes reconstructed by Dr Ur for archaeological research. There were approximately 150 mainly photographic flights over the region between 1956-60. (Map by George Anderson, based on E Hammer and J Ur, p.9)

Reworking U-2 Imagery Today

Our best insight into U-2 Middle East overflights comes via the world of ancient history. Archaeologists have long recognised the value of aerial photography for their discipline. In 2019 doctors Jason Ur and Emily Hammer published an article using declassified imagery from a number of U-2 missions over the region.[3] They identified film held at the US National Archive Record Administration (NARA) from 11 missions (four US and seven British) flown between 12 August 1958 and 29 January 1960. The imagery was deposited with NARA in 1997 and amounts to over 52,000 separate images – just a fraction of that shot during the duration of the programme. They very carefully documented the material held and reconstructed the data there into a useable form for their archaeological research. The reconstruction had to be done largely using secondary, contextual, data as the essential 'Finding Aids' were not declassified. Reconstructing individual mission routes was a major task for them. They described it as a very time-consuming, labour intensive exercise, as it indeed had been for the original NPIC Photo Interpreters.

To provide an illustration of the 'product' from these missions we primarily use just two examples: 'B1512' and 'B8652' in 1959. By then Middle East flights were largely repetitive, the relatively few important targets, mostly cities, ports and a few military locations had been repeatedly imaged. We get a very clear indication of this from a simple overlay Drs Ur and Hammer constructed from just the 11 flights they had access to. By 1959 these missions were largely about updating changes at existing installations and monitoring major troop movements. This may also explain why the imagery was declassified to NARA. There is little of military significance on it and declassification in 1997 probably presented few issues.

There were early problems for the British in particular with late changes to routes and rescheduling flights, as these had to be ratified by both British and US chains of command. It was believed that Macmillan would find it: 'tedious and irksome if called upon regularly to approve changes during the evening or overnight. Up until now, any changes have led to cancellation.' The solution was a form of limited 'block clearance'. Prime Ministerial approval was sought for several overflights with two alternative plans for each flight laid before the Foreign Secretary. This followed a similar pattern to US political approvals. Of the eight British Middle East flights approved for January only three were flown, the five cancellations attributed to weather. Macmillan's permission was simply sought to carry over the 'unused' flights to the following month, which was quickly granted.[4]

Middle East Photo Mission 1512

Mission 1512 was flown from Adana on 8 June 1959 by Marty Knutson in Art 352. We can see his route on the accompanying map. After take-off at 0400Z, he rapidly climbed to height to clear the contrail zone. His tracker camera was switched on for later post-flight route reconstruction. He flew over Syria, across northern Iraq and into Iran. As he progressed we can see the points where the camera was turned on and off. All the time he would have checked his navigation against the map coordinates on his planned route. His drift sight enabled him to track his precise route, barring cloud obscuring his view. In addition to camera on/off positions, pilots sometimes saw 'targets of opportunity'; then they would activate their cameras via a simple cockpit switch. Knutson used the B camera with its powerful 36-inch f/10 lens, set in Mode 1 for the whole flight. His ELINT Systems (Systems III and VI) were listening for radar or missile emissions, or VHF voice chatter. However, on this flight his System VI suffered a broken cable at the plug.[5] The pilot could do little more with these systems other than monitor the

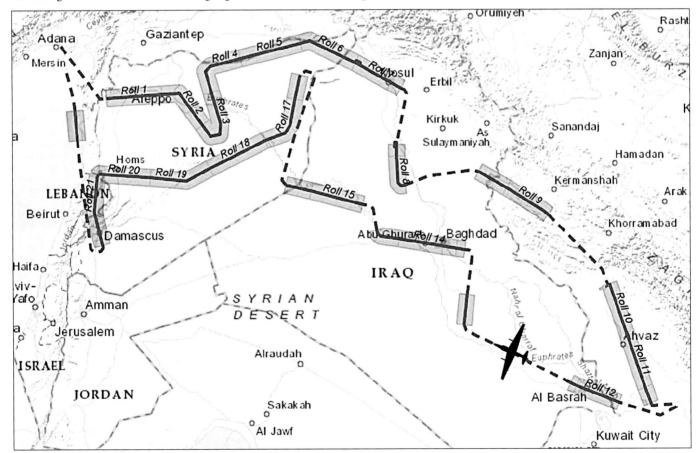

The route for Mission 1512, showing camera on (solid line) and off (broken) positions, plus approximate camera coverage and the roll numbers film was cut into after processing. (E Hammer and J Ur, p.7).

NAVIGATION IN THE EARLY U-2

A vital piece of equipment for the pilot was his drift sight. Linked to his sextant, this periscope system helped him maintain course and line up for key photographic targets. It sometimes even alerted him to the presence of MiGs below trying to intercept him. Marty Knutson has said: 'we had to fly a precise line at 70,000ft, looking through the drift sight and using maps. I'd compare what I was seeing through the sight to what the map showed. Pretty damned primitive, like 1930s flying, by the seat of the pants. But we all grew very skilled at it.'[11]

A 1959 CIA U-2 flight manual contains a simple diagrammatic representation of the system. The periscope pointed out below the outer skin of the U-2 inside a glass bubble on the underside of the aircraft. Inside the cockpit the pilot's restricted movement meant he could only lean forward to use a rubber sighting cone. This excluded extraneous light whilst flying during daylight, as the pilot observed the terrain below. The sight had two settings: single- and four-times magnification control. The scanning prism could be adjusted in both azimuth and elevation to give some flexibility. Later versions of the sight used an electrically powered hand control, mounted on the right cockpit console, to change the pilot's view. These rotated horizontally a full 360 degrees, looked directly beneath the aircraft or angled to either side of the aircraft.

Lieutenant Colonel Bruce Jinneman, a later SAC U-2R/TR-1 pilot explained how valuable it was:

The drift sight was pretty similar between C and R models. I thought it was fabulous. We had a 4x magnification and when looking straight down could see roughly 4-5 miles either side of our flight path with a hand control to swing it from horizon-to-horizon. On the C model, we sometimes practised High Flights (above 70,000 feet) following a Photo Flight Line (PFL, pronounced "Piffle"). For those, we had a track marked onto a map and once we got to our assigned height we followed the track without using any of our other navigation equipment. Everything was done just by time and heading. It was very easy to pick out features like cities, roads and dams, we got very comfortable flying with the view sight after a while. During training, we had to stay within two miles of that drift line, or we failed the flight.

Because in clear weather pilots could navigate so accurately, Bruce explained that the U-2s' Turn Points could be very precisely executed.

At high altitude you might have an Indicated Air Speed' of 98/100kts, with a ground speed of 350kts or so. You could comfortably roll the aircraft with 30-45 degrees of bank and turn the aircraft very smoothly. Say if you overflew a water tower and used it as your turn point you would still be within a mile or two of it by the time you completed the turn.

Lieutenant Colonel Rick Bishop, another SAC U-2 pilot, explained further:

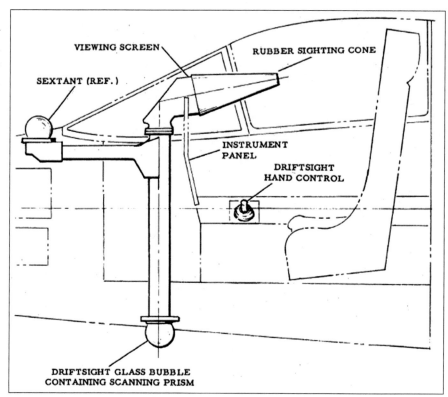

Flight manual representation of the U-2Cs drift sight, its hand control, pilot viewing screen and sextant. (CIA)

U-2 cockpit. The rubber cone allowed the pilot to lean forward slightly to look through his drift sight with reduced glare. (NASM)

Pilot's view of the cockpit, showing the drift sight viewer with its hood removed. (NASM)

The drift sight aka 'view sight' was the most accurate means of navigating until the advent of GPS and was even used to update the inertial navigation system (INS) on long flights in the U-2R. The view sight, used in conjunction with basic pilotage and dead-reckoning navigation was used until the glass cockpit of the U-2S came about in the 1990s.

Astro-Navigation

The sextant sits in a glass bubble just in front of the left side of the windscreen. It fed into the drift sight display using a simple mirror. Its optical system used a portion of the drift sight optics and was shown on the drift sight display.[12] Bruce Jinneman said of having to rely on astro-navigation: 'I give much credit to the pilots of the early U-2s having to navigate by shooting the stars, using astro-navigation, I just can't imagine how they managed

that.' U-2 pilot Lieutenant Colonel Rick Bishop described it in a little more detail: 'It was a complete nightmare, hated by all U-2 pilots.' Whilst an essential in the early days of CIA operations, by 1978 it was still a requirement that: 'all SAC aircraft be capable of navigating using celestial navigation, even U-2 pilots flying in the coffin corner at night, attempting to shoot three stars through the sextant and plotting a position that could easily be 20-miles off! Luckily, that procedure was dropped from training about a year before I arrived in the Programme.' It was still regarded as a last resort means of navigation in case nuclear weapons were detonated when the resulting electromagnetic pulse would have rendered all the electronic ground navigation aids useless.

Astro-navigation sextant protrudes through the U-2's upper surface. If a cloud undercast prevented sight of the ground, the sextant was the only means of visual navigation. (NASM)

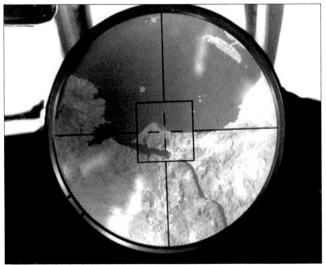

Through the drift sight, a view of the terrain below the U-2. The graticule marks approximately one square mile at operational altitudes. (Rick Bishop personal archive)

cockpit indicator light that told him if they were functioning. For most Middle East flights this equipment picked up little, if anything, as most flights went totally undetected.

The southernmost leg of Mission 1512 was planned to cover the northern Persian Gulf, tracing the Iranian coastline until close to Bandar, turning west to cross the Gulf continuing back up the coast before heading for targets in central Saudi Arabia.[6] His U-2 had begun to contrail, a specified mission abort condition.[7] At that point he cut short his route and headed westwards, resuming the remainder of the mission when the contrails ceased. In 1959 few aircraft flew at contrail height, so were an obvious giveaway, even if he was unseen by radar. The normal procedure saw U-2s climb as quickly as possible to a height above the usual contrail bracket (45,000ft to 55,000ft).[8] Normally this was done before entering denied airspace. To contrail at Knutson's recorded 66,000ft altitude was very unusual, possibly caused by the large temperature differences between the desert landscape and the waters of the Persian Gulf.

As Knutson progressed he would have periodically recorded his altitude, and exhaust gas temperature and made sure he was still within his flight fuel curve to enable him to reach home. He landed safely back at Adana at 1115Z with an elapsed flight time of 7hrs 15mins. After landing the aircraft was checked over, Knutson debriefed and equipment defects reported. The film was carefully extracted from the cameras and would have been packaged for transport to one of the photo processing locations – in Germany or the US. The 700 frames from the 70mm tracker film were developed locally.[9] The speed with which the film was picked up from Adana depended on the mission's priority. Sometimes several missions were combined and transported together. The 'take' from this flight was due to be taken with that from two further flights scheduled for a few days later. That plan suffered a partial setback when Knutson's 12 June mission (1514 in Art 352), had to be abandoned over Egypt after a cockpit seal failed and caused depressurisation, two hours after take-off. On the same day, British flight 8629 did not take-off after approval was not received from the MoD and was substituted by CIA Mission 1515. High priority mission 'take' was immediately whisked back to the US, normally via West Germany.

The materials were couriered by air, usually to Westover AFB, MA. From there they were processed either by Eastman Kodak or the Air Force Special Processing Production Facility (AFSPPF) at Westover AFB.[10] Processing and copying for 1512 began on 14 June at 0415hrs and completed at 1430hrs. By the following morning, it was being delivered to NPIC and later in the day to customers in Washington DC and elsewhere.

Emergency Landing Locations

It was suggested that if a U-2 had to force-land in Egypt, Syria, Iraq, Afghanistan or Yemen the pilots should eject from the aircraft, or destroy it on the ground, using the small explosive charge it carried and undertake 'escape and evasion'. But if they needed to force-land in Israel, Lebanon, Iran, Jordan, Pakistan, Aden, Sudan, Eritrea, Libya, Tunisia or Algeria the aircraft need not be destroyed. In Saudi Arabia's case they recommended that if it was flown by a British pilot the aircraft should be destroyed but that an American pilot might seek assistance.[13] Several airfields were even suggested as possible emergency diversions: Nicosia (Cyprus), Beirut (Lebanon), Tel

Table 3: Selected overflights close to Dimona and Negev Research Centre			
Date	Msn No.	Camera	Approximate closest approach distance to Dimona and Negev Research Centre, respectively
30 Nov 1956	1340	A2	14 and 7 NM
29 June 1958	1421	B	5 and 10 NM
10 January 1959	8604	B	41 and 34 NM

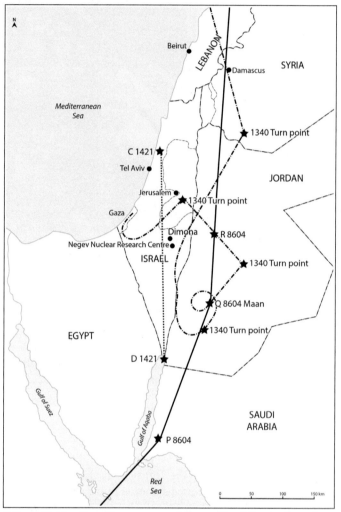

U-2 overflights of Israel became especially sensitive following its early nuclear research efforts and after construction began in the Negev desert. This map shows portions of the approximate routes from three selected flights, known to have flown close to Dimona. There were others. Table 3 estimates the closest approach distances of the known flights close to Dimona and the Negev Research Centre. (Map by George Anderson, based on CIA data)

Aviv (Israel), El Adem (Libya), Amman (Jordan), Dhahran (Saudi Arabia), Kermanshah (Iran), Abadan (Iran), Wadihalfa (Sudan) or any field in Turkey.

Lebanon Flights 1958

There was a surge of U-2 Middle East missions during the summer of 1958 as political instabilities rocked the region again and the U-2 was employed in a set of 'tactical' overflights. There was concerted action between Syria and Egypt in the region, through their brief 'union' following the United Arab Republic's creation in 1958. Lebanon and Jordan came under particular pressure, including the threat of coups, invasion and perhaps wider war with Israel. In July the situation became especially parlous and Lebanon's President Camille Chamoun invited western intervention in the country.

On July 15 the first US Marines arrived in Lebanon and the British mounted a similar stabilisation operation in Jordan.

This major intensification in U-2 overflights of Syria, Lebanon, Jordan and Egypt started with six in the latter half of June. Flights hit a peak with 20 in July and 11 more in August. They tapered down to just three in September, with the last US troops withdrawing on 25 October. There were two U-2 flights in October and three more in November. Dino Brugioni has explained these missions were used to support US troop deployments in the region. Eisenhower said of these 36 flights that they were like having a 'guardian angel watching over them.'[14] The coverage was so extensive that by the end of July ARC's chairman James Reber noted that images from around a third of the missions were processed but not printed, or distributed, to 'customers' instead retained at HTAUTOMAT in case they were required at a later date.[15]

Many of these missions were mounted against Syrian airfields and army camps where Soviet equipment was expected to be delivered. Locations imaged included: Hamah airfield, Dimashq Barracks and the Qatana ammunition depot, plus newly identified airfields at Esriye, Saygal and Deir Ez Zoir South and Lebanon's Beirut international airport.[16] During the period a small number of flights went as far afield as Iraq, Iran, Saudi Arabia and Kuwait, but these were more a continuation of routine operations, beyond the immediate emergency.

Israel

Collecting U-2 overflight imagery of Israel was always a sensitive issue for their government, certainly some of it at least attributable to the construction of the nuclear research reactor at Dimona and suspected underground chemical weapons or processing facilities in the Negev. Although never discussed in declassified material, Dino Brugioni has asserted that Eisenhower was well aware of the extent of Israel's nuclear programme. This is evidenced in his description of how he and Art Lundhal saw imagery of growing spoil heaps at the site, unmistakable signs of reactor construction and the erection of fences around 1958–59. How what they saw was most definitely kept out of written reports and how there were never any requests for further details of the area.[17] We can get further indication that the facilities were imaged from a few Mission Coverage Plots of some Middle East flights. Several passed within a few miles of Dimona and the Negev research site, certainly within camera range.[18]

Although the level of U-2 aerial surveillance of the Negev research site prior to May 1960 may be difficult to pin down there are some satellite images available. The quality of the imagery from 1968 and

Table 4: Det B British Middle East Flights						
Msn No.	Date	Art No.	Pilot	Countries overflown	Kit	Notes
8603B	31 Dec 58	367	McArthur	Syria, Egypt, Jordan	B	
8604B	10 Jan 59	352	Bradley	Syria, Egypt, Saudi Arabia, Jordan, Lebanon	B	
8605B	13 Jan 59	352	Dowling	Syria, Saudi Arabia, Iraq, Kuwait	B	
8608B	20 Jan 59	355	Robinson	Syria, Egypt, Saudi Arabia	B	
8618B	21 Mar 59	367	Bradley	Syria	B	
8620B	26 Mar 59	351	Dowling	Egypt	B	Aborted
8625B	16 Apr 59	367	Robinson	Syria, Saudi Arabia, Jordan	B	
8626B	20 May 59	352	Bradley	Egypt	B	
8627B	04 Jun 59	352	Bradley	Egypt	B	
8630B	26 Jun 59	355	N/K	Syria	B	Aborted
8631B	27 Jun 59	367	McArthur	Syria, Iraq, Lebanon	B	
8632B	16 Jul 59	355	Robinson	Syria, Saudi Arabia, Iraq	B	
8634B	07 Aug 59	355	Dowling	Syria, Saudi Arabia, Iraq, Iran	B	
8636B	28 Aug 59	367	Bradley	Syria, Iraq, Iran	B	
8638B	10 Sep 59	367	Bradley	Syria, Saudi Arabia, Iraq, Kuwait, Lebanon, Iran	B	
8648B	30 Oct 59	367	Dowling	Syria, Saudi Arabia, Iraq, Kuwait, Iran	B	
8649B	30 Oct 59	344	McArthur	Syria, Egypt, Saudi Arabia, Jordan, Iraq, Lebanon	B	
8652B	19 Nov 59	367	McArthur	Syria, Jordan, Iraq, Lebanon, Iran	B	
8004B	20 Nov 59	344	Dowling	Afghanistan	Sys VII	R7 launch Baikonour
8007B	06 Dec 59	n/k	Bradley	Iran	Sys IV	Diversionary HIGH WIRE
HS501	27 Jan 60	344	Bradley	Iran	Sys VII	
HS503	31 Jan 60	344	Robinson	Iran	Sys VII	R7A launch Baikanour
8010B	05 Feb 60	n/k	Dowling	Iran	Sys IV	Diversionary KNIFE EDGE
Total:	23					
(Based on CIA records) NB. Excludes Soviet overflights 8005B and 8009B						

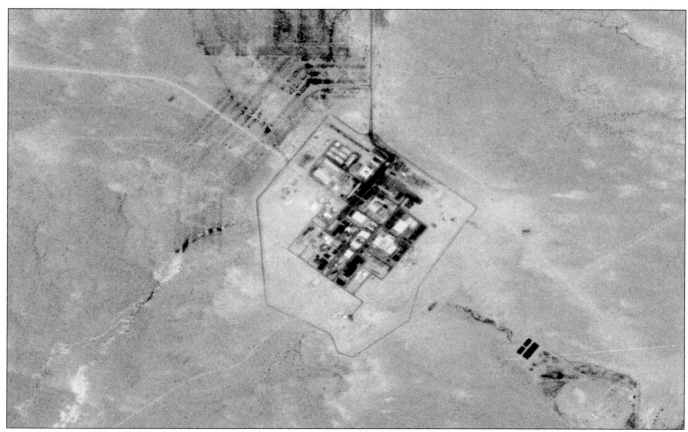

The Negev reactor site from KH-4B Mission 1103 7 May 1968, showing the extent of the now well-developed research facility, but rather fuzzy detail. (CAST)

Same site from Mission 1110 on 8 June 1970, was significantly over exposed and required major manipulation to make it printable here but showing significantly sharper focus. (CAST)

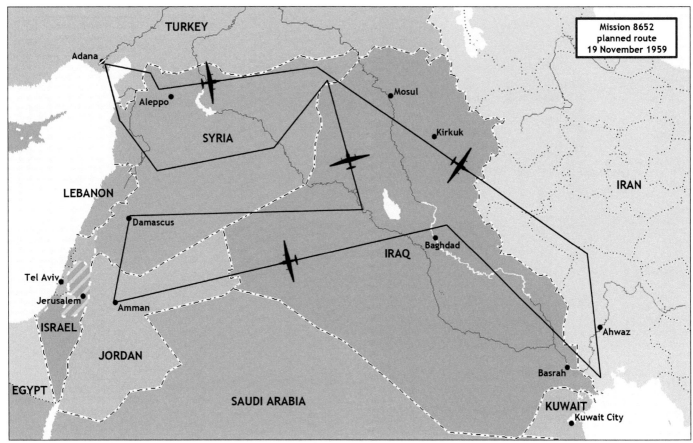

Planned coordinates for Mission 8652. (Map by Tom Cooper, based on CIA data)

1970 allows the main reactor dome and other large features to be seen, but lacks in detail. From Brugioni's detailed descriptions of the site in 1958-59 it is reasonable to deduce that the U-2 imagery must have been of a much finer quality.

Everyday practical technical considerations caused frequent frustrations for analysts too. A satellite pass from another mission, on 26 September 1967, sees the end of the frame exactly bisect the entire reactor site and looks like just a badly out of focus smudge of no practical value.

British Middle East Flights

Middle East flights were of importance to British regional interests. They were also of considerable training value with the British eager to begin Soviet overflights. Ministry of Defence files opened in 2019 related to British U-2 operations provided more details about the RAF's 18 operational Middle East overflights. Many of the documents in these files are teletype messages passed via the CIA/USAF HBJAYWALK network. The CIA used a large number of cryptonyms that have to be understood to make sense of the messages.[19]

A memo to the RAF Vice Chief of the Air Staff from Air Vice-Marshal John Grandy (cryptonym KWCROWN-7) outlined preparations for the first RAF missions. It sought a programme of six overflights of the Soviet Union during the first three months of 1959.[20] There was haste on the British side to get the first flights underway. A U-2 returned to Adana from RAF Watton just before Christmas 1958 after their unsuccessful efforts to mount some meteorological flights. The first operational British mission was planned for 31 December 1958 (8603). John MacArthur ventured over Egypt, Syria and Jordan. The MoD files reveal this as very much a shakedown period in preparation for Soviet overflights.

Mission 8652

This overflight on 19 November 1959, was made by RAF pilot Flt Lt John MacArthur in Art 367, taking off at 0435Z. It turned out to be the last British Middle East overflight from Det B up to their withdrawal following Gary Powers' loss on 1 May 1960. MacArthur's route initially took him across Syria, then along the Iran-Iraq border. This area was, and remained, important to the British, having recently been expelled from Iraq following the 14 July 1958 revolution. He turned towards Kuwait before heading back into Iraq via Basrah to Baghdad, across Iraq into Jordan. Intriguingly, much of the mission's actual flightpath deviated from the planned route. This is particularly true of the very meandering course from Points F to H and again near the Point of Exit. The significant difference between the two is as yet unaccounted for. It raises possibilities of equipment failure, a change in mission objectives through to simple pilot spatial disorientation. He arrived back at Adana 8hrs 10mins later. During the overflight McArthur's tracker camera took 985 images and 3275 images – over 4,912ft of film from the main camera magazines.[21]

Missile Hunting

Another high priority for Det B U-2 operations became intercepting communications and electronic emissions gathering missile telemetry intelligence (TELINT) from Soviet missile facilities and test launches. It was an effort that involved the US Army, Navy, Air Force, NSA and Adana based CIA U-2s.

By 1955 a number of missile test launch sites were either suspected, or already positively identified. Tyuratam, today's Baikanour Cosmodrome in Kazakhstan, was under construction. Three other locations soon became the highest priority targets: Plesetsk in the Arkhangelsk Oblast of north-western Russia,

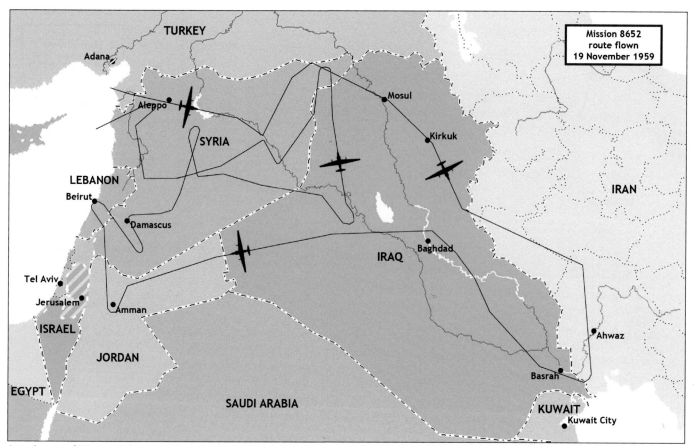

Actual route of Mission 8652, comparison shows significant deviations especially between points F to H. The deviation is as yet unexplained. (Map by Tom Cooper, based on E Hammer and J Ur, p.7)

Kapustin Yar in the south between the Black and Caspian seas and Sary Shagan in eastern Kazakhstan.

A significant number of dedicated U-2 ELINT flights were aimed at these targets. Designed by HRB-Singer, System VII was an automated collection system installed in the U-2's 'Q-Bay.' The Ampex 814 Recorder could record up to 12 minutes of data simultaneously from six different frequencies. Assembled by the end of 1958, it was tested at Edwards AFB then quickly sent to Turkey. Art 344 (56-6677), the only U-2 fitted with System VII and the original U-2 J-57 engine. Using a newer J-75 powered equipped aircraft would have required modification to 344s electrical wiring

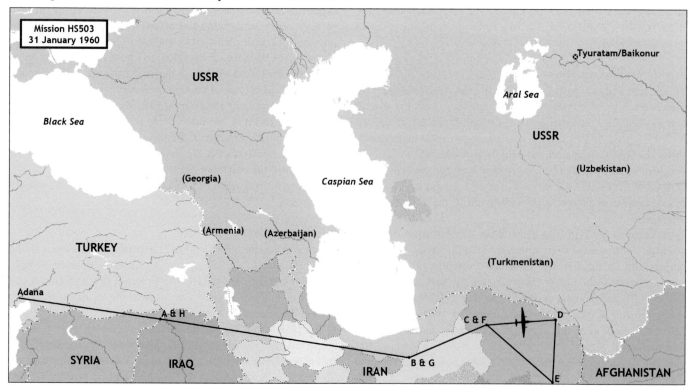

Attempting to track Soviet missile launches was an important part of Det Bs work. Missions like HS503 used a set track, well clear of the border areas, so Soviet radar could not track them. (Map by Tom Cooper, based on Landsat, SIO, USN, NGA, NOAA, GEBCO)

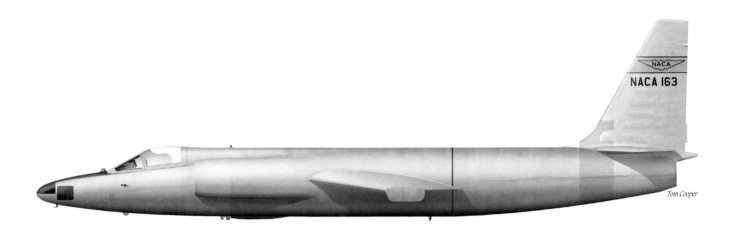

U-2A 'NACA 163' flew Mission 2023 from Wiesbaden on 10 July 1956, piloted by Glen Dunaway. Equipped with an 'A' camera, the 2,042-mile round trip took him over the GDR, Poland, into Soviet Ukraine, the Black Sea, returning via Romania, Hungary, Czechoslovakia and the GDR again. The U-2A's early natural metal finish was replaced by an overall dark blue from around mid-1957. (Artwork by Tom Cooper)

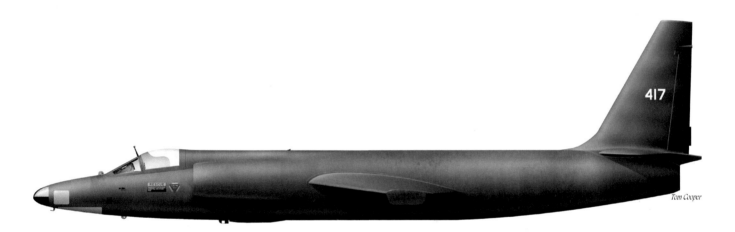

On 7 and 8 May 1959, Art 349 flew two 'meteorological flights' from RAF Watton, Norfolk. The simple 'Weather Package' recorded airspeed, altitude, external air temperature and humidity. The flights were really cover for a test of Detachment B's ability to mount 'Fast Move' deployments to remote air bases. The application of false serial numbers was a regular procedure. (Artwork by Tom Cooper)

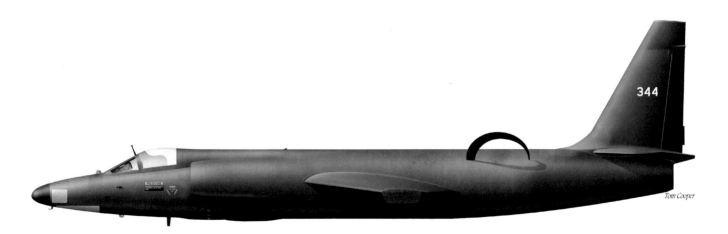

The ineffective Ramshorn antenna on the rear fuselage was associated with HRB-Singer's System VII. U-2A Art 344 was the only aircraft fitted with the equipment, developed to collect telemetry from Soviet missile launches and used for 23 operational missions. Art 344 retained its original J-57 engine rather than the J-75. Installation of the newer J-75 would have required substantial modifications to prevent electrical interference to System VII's listening and recording equipment. (Artwork by Tom Cooper)

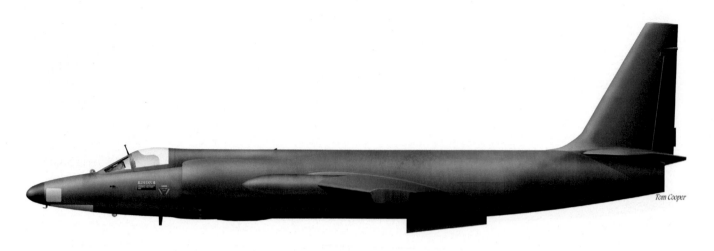

Operation 'High Wire' was the first British-flown deep penetration mission into the USSR. Launched from Peshawar in Pakistan, Mission 8005 used Art 351 on 6 December 1959 it was piloted by Squadron Leader 'Robbie' Robinson. The aircraft was totally unmarked, carried a B camera and the ventral fin associated with the System VI SIGINT equipment. (Artwork by Tom Cooper)

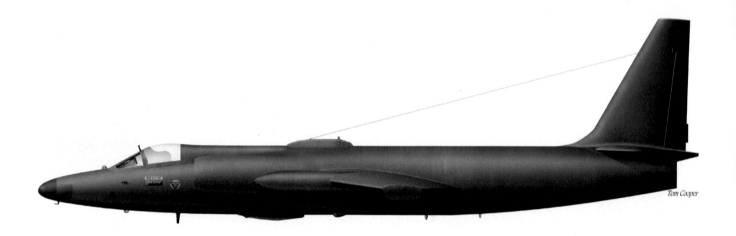

The U-2C's spine became a key location for mounting important electronic equipment items. One of the first was a small fuselage 'bump' behind the cockpit. This housed an early Collins 180L-3 automatic HF antenna tuner for some of the onboard radio equipment and required a wire antenna. (Artwork by Tom Cooper)

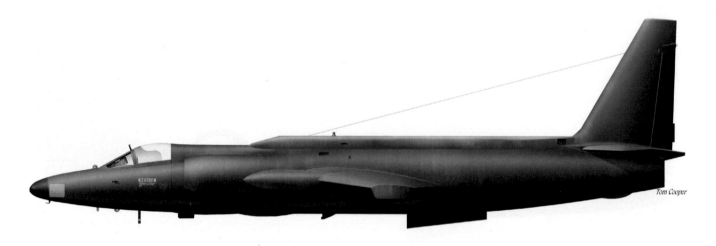

The specially developed, pressurised 'long spine' could accommodate up to 100lb loads and was fitted to the non-air refuelling equipped U-2Cs. Equipment was added and removed as required, one of the most important being System IX. Developed by Granger from 1958 it was intended to generate 'false angles' to fool enemy radars and missiles about the U-2's real position. It also housed the Collins 618-T3 HF single sideband radio, navigation light and HF wire antenna. (Artwork by Tom Cooper)

From East Sale in Australia in May 1961, fully marked, USAF-operated U-2s flew fallout sampling missions. Photographed at East Sale air show, this example was shown with the payload package removed from the Q-Bay. (Eric Allen)

Art 383, 'Armed Forces Special Weapons Project' with its hard nose U-2 for radioactive sampling and the externally mounted P-2 fallout collection equipment. (USAF)

U-2C Art 349 (56-6682) had a very distinguished flying career. It flew operationally, as a Dirty Bird, was converted to the unique H model, reverted to a G and flew with NASA from 1971 until retiring in 1989. (CIA)

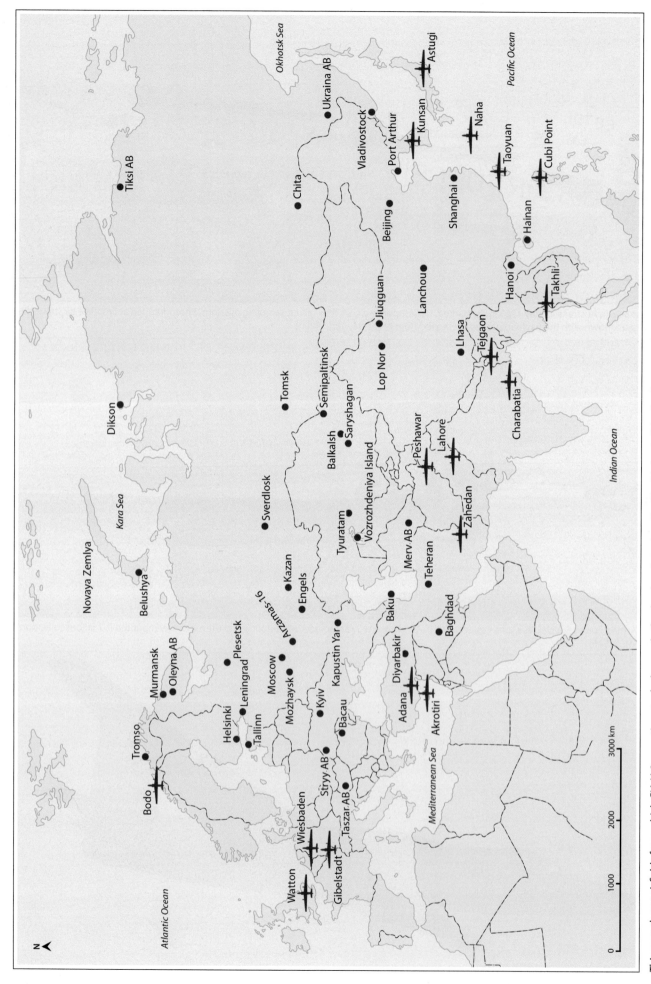

This map shows airfields from which CIA U-2 operations took place and other key locations described in this book. (Map by George Anderson)

CAMERA IMAGERY

Dr Jason Ur kindly provided a few samples of imagery from the Middle East missions he digitised for his research. The quality is still astounding today.

Mission 8652, piloted by Flt Lt John McArthur. The central oval feature is the Aleppo Citadel Grand Mosque. The U-2's Hycon B camera used a 36-inch lens and could resolve features as small as 2.5 ft from 65,000ft in ideal conditions. (Jason Ur/US NARA)

This is the Iraqi city of Nineveh on the River Tigris, today part of Mosul. Taken on 30 October 1959 by Flt Lt David Dowling during Mission 8648 using the B camera. (Jason Ur/US NARA)

This is a tracker camera image from Mission 8649, flown by Flt Lt John McArthur on 30 October 1959. The shot looks south down the Nile from Cairo. (Jason Ur/US NARA)

Specially equipped Sea Brine EA-3Bs hunted for missile telemetry with Adana based U-2s. (Akira Watanabe)

to prevent interference with the System VII equipment.[22] It was used by Det B, for 23 flights during 1959-60.

SAC used its own specially modified 'Tell Two' EB-47E(TT)s. These carried manually operated tuners and flew at much lower altitudes than the U-2. The US Navy was also involved using its more basically equipped, specially modified 'Sea Brine' EA-3Bs, manned by US Army crews for this operation. All were competing to try and collect relevant data at the same time. The first success with System VII came with the launch of an R-7 missile from Baikanour on 9 June 1959. Art 344 and a SAC Tell Two worked together in a joint mission. US ground sites in Turkey gave approximately six hours prior warning of launches. This enabled the EB-47E(TT) to

be patrolling at 35,000ft when the R-7 launched at 2034Z, around 675nm distant from its patrol orbit. The U-2 'Mission 4120' was flown by pilot James Barnes. His 9hr 25min flight saw him climb to around 65,000ft flying in Turkish, Iranian and Afghan airspace, close to the Soviet border. His System VII detected signals about 80 seconds after the missile launch, capturing around 30 seconds of telemetry up to the burnout of the R-7s first stage. The Tell Two EB-47Es used manual frequency searching and flew lower, so took longer to acquire the missile's transmissions but recorded the second stage firing sequence that complemented the U-2 data. Ground radars, such as the USAFSS site at Diyarbakir in Turkey, played a major part too from 1955. They detected launches from Kapustin

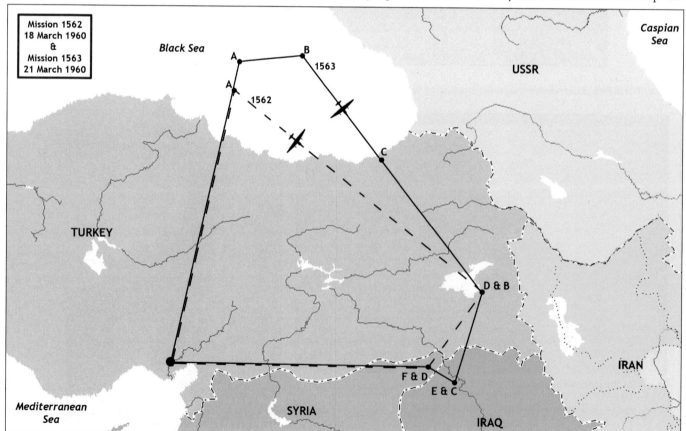

Missions 1562 and 1563. U-2 TELINT were accompanied by similar USAF and USN operations from Adana. These missions were often far from successful with significant numbers of missile launch delays and cancellations that gave long missions for literally a few minutes data. (Map by Tom Cooper based on Landsat, SIO, USN, NGA, NOAA, GEBCO)

The specially modified EB-47(TT)s, with box mounted aerials, worked at much lower altitudes than the Det B U-2s to collect missile telemetry. (John Kovacs via Robert Hopkins)

Yar and by 1958 the detected signals from a second antenna array could be displayed on oscilloscopes, which were photographed on 35mm film and sent back to Wright Patterson AFB for exploitation.[23]

In addition to CIA crews, RAF pilots participated in these TELINT missions: Flt Lt David Dowling on 20 November 1959 (8004), Flt Lt Michael Bradley on 27 January 1960 (HS501) and Squadron Leader Robbie Robinson on 31 January 1960 (HS503). From January 1960 these TELINT flights had been renamed 'Hot Shop' missions. Most of the System VII flights operated around a set track known as 'Route A.' This took them from Adana to the Syrian/Iraq border near the city of Rabia, then across northern Iran, 55nm south of the Caspian, over the city of Semnan, turning south near Mashad, close to the Soviet (Turkmenistan) border. Still no closer than 550nm to the Tyuratam/Baikonur launch site it paralleled the Afghan border before turning again near the village of Mazabad, in the Khaf district and heading back to Seman and retracing its route back to Turkey. Details of these missions were also passed to the US Ambassador in Iran in case of an incident.[24]

Squadron Leader Robbie Robinson, the British Detachment commander, discussed the U-2's role in telemetry collection during a 1993 interview with Paul Lashmar:

For the rocket launches we carried an entirely different configuration. It was a giant recorder. We were not the only people involved – [there was also] the US Navy and SAC. Despite three or four detachments in the same place, nobody told anyone else what they were doing. But it was significant that we all took off on the same day![25]

Whilst some missions were successful, significant numbers were not. The U-2's System VII equipment, then advanced technology, suffered major problems including sometimes severe internal system noise, inadequate sensitivity, limited range, automatic tape activation and recording quality issues. The System's original

use of 'Ramshorn' aerials was problematic, as they exhibited poor performance at detecting low power signals over these extreme distances. Even when it worked, launch data would often be only partially recorded and was not always of decipherable quality. This was highlighted in a March 1960 report which described that the recorder was switched on 90 seconds after launch but that data between 2min 30sec and 3min 20sec was not useable because the equipment needed improved sensitivity adjustment.

There were two more System VII flights: on 18 March 1960 (1562) piloted by Bob Ericson and on 21 March 1960 (1563) Jake Kratt in Art 344.[26] Kratt's flight reached further north, closer to the Soviet coast, than Ericson's mission. The coordinates from these routes indicate just how distant these flights actually operated from Soviet borders. Intended to keep the U-2s out of Soviet radar range it meant that they were no closer than 430nm from the Kapustin Yar launch site. The importance of keeping at least 25nm from Soviet border was stressed, concerned it might provoke an adverse Soviet reaction that could affect other aircraft, presumably the EB-47TTs and Sea Brine EA-3Bs.[27] The technical difficulties of mounting successful flights is highlighted in a letter from HRB-Singer: 'Adding to the problems of making these intercepts are the facts that the intercept is usually made at extreme ranges and from poor positions.' It additionally mentions that in some instances the 'Ramshorn' antenna on the U-2s were so ineffective that useful information could not be extracted.[28] The take from Mission 1562 was said to be inadequate, consisting of 20 individual 'lock ons' by Soviet radars averaging just 20 seconds each.[29]

5

SOVIET SKIES

By late 1958 convergent factors were placing great pressures on CIA overflights of the Soviet Union. At the public level, far away from the CHALICE programme, fears were growing about Russian capabilities, especially given Khruschev's ever more boastful claims about its nuclear weapons and missiles. Within US domestic politics there were demands from Congress, the armed services and large defence industrial companies for vast funding increases to counter perceived growing Soviet advantage. For those select few in the intelligence community, with access to the CHALICE programme, they were searching for solid data on Soviet nuclear facilities, bomber bases, missile and space programmes. The vast Soviet hinterland remained largely an intelligence 'black hole.'

The simple fact that U-2 overflights had been so readily detected and tracked was a significant early blow to the programme. US reputation was somewhat damaged by detailed public Soviet protests about overflights. The U-2's photographic, and increasingly electronic, sensors were yielding improving results, but the aircraft's ever-growing weight was gradually impairing its performance. Soviet air defences were advancing rapidly too, especially with the development of the SA-2 and improved organisation. Technical advances, especially an improved engine, pushed the U-2's operating altitude a little higher but inevitably that bar on the window of opportunity for overflights was closing. Deep penetration missions required ever more careful planning to avoid SA-2 SAM sites and employ tactics to confuse, or mislead Soviet air defences about U-2 launch fields, their highest priority targets and likely approach routes.

The southern arc of Soviet republics had become ever more important target areas, but their air defences were constantly being improved. Flights in the Soviet Far East were largely limited to the Kamchatka peninsula, a few airbases and naval facilities plus some industrial presence. To the west, in Europe, U-2s were easily tracked and overflights protested. It was along the USSR's vast northern coastline and the hinterland from Murmansk, down to Leningrad that American attention turned.

Norway and U-2 Staging Operations

The admitted details of Norway's role in the U-2 story have always been rather vague, but it was certainly much greater than the generally passive role admitted. Colonel Vilhelm Evang, Head of Norway's Intelligence Service, played a pivotal role in his country's involvement with the U-2. An often controversial figure, described as determined and reluctant to delegate, he frequently had major conflicts with senior colleagues.[1] His critical role was in facilitating US access to Norwegian bases for U-2 missions. In return, this helped Norway secure finance, equipment, training and access to the intelligence product from U-2 activities and other wide-ranging operations in which the country became involved.

There have since been accusations that Evang did not ensure senior politicians and military staff were adequately briefed about US operations for them to give sufficiently well-informed consent to U-2 activities from Norway. Evang accused the CIA in particular of not being frank about the missions they wanted to undertake. However, that assessment sounds as if he was being rather economical with the truth. There appears no deliberate attempt to deceive the Norwegians into allowing U-2 flights from its bases. It more

readily appears that Evang perhaps took too much responsibility on himself, failing to adequately engage with his own government and military leadership. Equally senior US officials failed to ensure that the multiple linkages usually exercised with the Norwegians at government, military and intelligence agency levels were properly worked. Indeed, some of these issues are expressed by the CIA in its own history of U-2 operations.[2] Given the close relationship between the US and Norwegians on intelligence matters, there was no obvious excuse for any accidental liaison failure.

On 13 September 1957, an ARC meeting discussed priorities for upcoming missions from Bodø to which the Norwegians had agreed. Options considered included a peripheral mission to capture naval activities, an overflight of the Novaya Zemlya nuclear

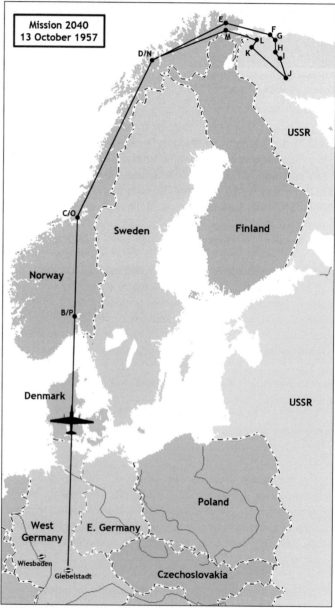

Mission 2040 pushed the limit of the U-2's endurance. It followed an overland route across Norway in contradiction to some published accounts. (Map by Tom Cooper based on Landsat/Copernicus, SIO, NOAA, USN, NGA, GEBCO, IBCAO, USGS).

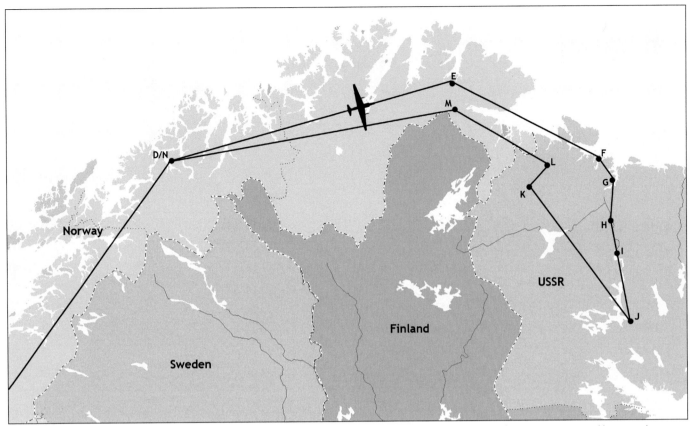

Close up of the overflight portion of 2040, skirting close to Finnish airspace. Its most valuable imagery came from numerous naval bases and a nuclear weapons store. The U-2 was pursued by MiG-17s and MiG-19s that attempted to intercept it. (Map by Tom Cooper based on CIA data)

testing ground and imaging naval installations around Severomorsk and Severodinsk. Novaya Zemlya was ruled out because of the sun angle. Trying to successfully intercept the Soviet Northern Fleet, whilst it was at sea, to collect imagery was considered too difficult.[3] In autumn 1957 two final operational missions were authorised for the declining Detachment A, now at Giebelstadt in West Germany before it closed. The first was an ELINT flight, Mission 2037 (see Chapter 2) over the Barents Sea on 11 October 1957 during Soviet naval exercises. This involved the first operational use of 'System IV' COMINT equipment to detect fleet transmissions.[4]

That was followed on 13 October 1957 by Mission 2040, using Art 351 again, but now with an A2 camera configuration with its 24-inch lens and tracking camera. Piloted by Harvey Stockman, this was the last mission from Gibelstadt. Filled with 1,525 gallons of JP-5 fuel, Stockman took off at 0535Z in thick fog. Heading north, he climbed to height, with a thick undercast below. Only over Norway did the cloud briefly break.

A fuel counter carefully measured the precise amount used, having been set to the exact amount of fuel in the aircraft after it was refuelled and before take-off. As the aircraft reached its designated turn points the pilot recorded the fuel remaining on the green card in his cockpit. Stockman experienced difficulties with the cockpit air conditioning and fluctuating engine exhaust gas temperatures, which could signify higher than predicted fuel consumption. The cockpit became so hot he had to pull the circuit breaker to reset the air conditioning. Even as he reached point Echo, just before leaving Norwegian airspace, he was 92 gallons behind his fuel curve – more than 300 nautical miles of JP-5. The crewman who set the fuel counter had wrongly set it at only 500 gallons. In reality, Stockman was only 57 gallons down, but he did not know it.

At 0902Z Stockman turned east, clear of the north Norwegian coast, and was detected by Soviet radars. Concerned about the apparent shortfall in fuel and with cloud ahead, he decided to miss point Foxtrot instead passing over Severomorsk and just east of Murmansk.[5] It was the port facilities, naval vessels, airfields and myriad of other installations that were the overflights top priority. Stockman reported seeing contrails of aircraft below. A Norwegian account confirms this mission was subject to numerous attempted intercepts by MiG-17 and MiG-19 fighters.[6] After passing east of Monechegorsk, Stockman turned north-west. He left Soviet airspace 'about 15nm west of the Rybachiy Peninsula at approximately 1100Z and headed west up Norway's Veranger Fjord'.[7] This route took him marginally clear of Finnish airspace. He passed back over the Norwegian interior and returned to Gibelstadt. Dino Brugioni has described the mission as successfully covering naval bases at Polyarny, Sada Guba, Olenyya Guba, Severomorsk and Murmansk, identifying several naval vessels, airfields, aircraft, radars and a secure area, believed to be the first Soviet naval nuclear weapon storage area.[8] Later disclosed accounts of the mission route have been disingenuous. In an early Agency U-2 history, one map plots 2040 as being mounted from Germany flying outside Norwegian airspace from Germany, off Norway's coast and round North Cape to enter the Barents Sea.[9]

The Norwegians claimed that its Defence Intelligence Staff had no prior knowledge of the mission only learning about it when its ground stations monitored Soviet air defence responses to the U-2.[10] Following this mission, Allen Dulles sent a personal telegram to Evang apologising for the incursion.[11] One cannot help but feel rather cynical about that apology, given that the routing was directly over Oslo, Trondheim and Tromsø. It was perhaps more a question of which Norwegians knew about the flight and had given their permission. The CIA perhaps thought it was necessary to 'protect' Evang's position. A more conspiratorial viewpoint suggests that perhaps this was utilised by Evang to apply leverage after the event.

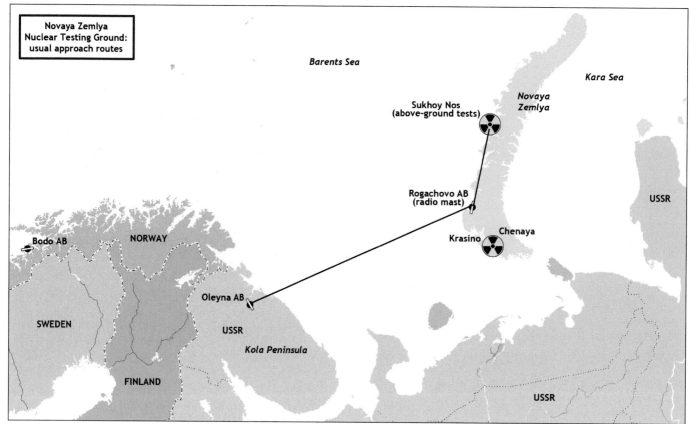

Novaya Zemlya nuclear testing ground is in the far north. For air-drop tests Soviet Badger bombers departed Olenya AB, south of Murmansk, flew across the Barents Sea and over Rogachevo airfield. They dropped nuclear weapons on the Sukhoy Nos peninsula, including the massive 58 megaton 'Tsar Bomba' on 30 October 1961. Other above-ground test sites included Chenaya and Krasino to the south of the island all used between 1957-62. (Map by Tom Cooper based on CIA data)

He could have reasoned that Norwegian governmental protests might persuade the Americans to supply them with hard copies of this mission imagery, which they later did. The US offer was made on 15 November, accepted by the Norwegians 'with appreciation, promising support for future operations if ever required.'[12] Dino Brugioni details that the CIA helped the Norwegians establish a photo interpretation capability for U-2 imagery via Sid Stallings, Special Assistant to Lundahl.[13]

A US approach to the Norwegians for airfield use was not long coming. On 19 June 1958 CIA Colonel Beerli (Det B Commander) visited Bodø and Andøya air bases to look at the facilities, settling for the former. Subsequently, several flights were agreed. Codenamed 'Honeymoon' they were abandoned following the shooting down of a US C-118 over Armenia on 27 June 1958.[14] Missions related to the Lebanon crisis then became a short-term American priority over the summer.[15]

A combination of CIA documents and Norwegian sources give us some insight into a significant series of missions originating from Norway planned for the autumn of 1958.

Operation 'New Moon' has been discussed as encompassing ELINT missions and overflights and caused clear tensions between the Agency and the USAF. US Colonel William Burke, CIA Deputy Project Director, briefed the Air Staff on 2 September 1958 about proposed coverage of the Polyarny Urals. Eisenhower had expressed the wish that the mission launch from Norway. Norwegian approval was given on 4 September 1958. A Norwegian account suggests that the stated purpose of 'Babyface' (as they knew it) 'was meteorological observations over international waters in the northern area. It had advance approval from the Cabinet Defence and Security Committee. It involved two U-2 planes.' Later, a Norwegian Defence Staff memorandum indicated that the original plan had been for one

or two flights from Bodø along the northern Soviet rim to Alaska and back for 'various intelligence purposes.'[16]

Norwegian historian Rolf Tamnes has provided substantive detail on some of the activities. He outlined that the Norwegian officials who approved the deployment were a very small group. He suggested that around six people knew of it in Oslo intelligence circles, two Royal Norwegian Air Force senior officers at Bodø (excluding the Air Force Regional Commander or Station Commander). One of those was Wg Cdr Just Ebbesen who had responsibility for intelligence flights in the north – including allied missions – and acted as liaison and support for the U-2 flights. Tamnes says that between 28 August and 9 September 11 C-130, five C-54 and one C-119 flight passed through Bodø in preparation for the U-2's arrival. The CIA party included Beerli, four pilots (including Gary Powers), 8–10 technicians and a security officer.[17] The delayed arrival of two U-2s and more personnel on 15 September 1958 was attributed to 'weather delays and aircraft faults.'[18] Arriving via different routes, one aircraft flew over southern Norway, the other entered Norwegian airspace from the north. Both U-2s were housed in a revetted earth-covered hangar.[19]

Continued bad weather caused further delays and route modification to the planned mission. There were near-daily 'negative alerts' (cancellations), mostly due to weather, from 20 September through to 25 October 1958. Gary Powers' memoirs briefly mention this deployment to Bodø in the 'fall of 1958' and indicates the aircraft were unable to fly for most of the time due to bad weather.[20] Chris Pocock mentions one flight on 9 October from Bodø around the Barents Sea using the P-2 sampling equipment for nuclear fallout collection which lasted 7hrs 55mins.[21] This is probably Mission 1482, unusually for flights in this numbering sequence, no details

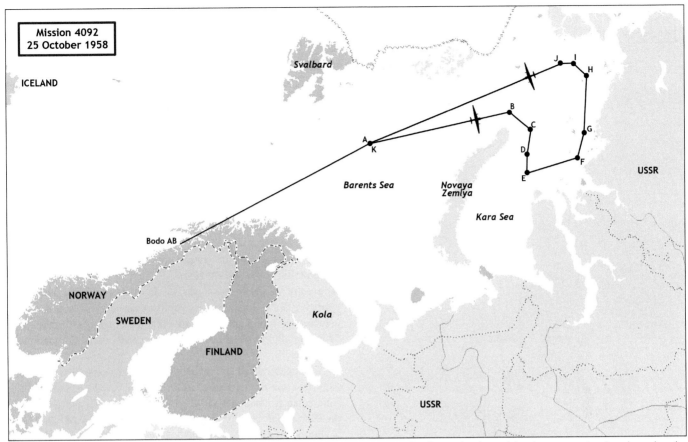

Mission 4092 was an ambitious operation into the High Arctic, skirting around Yuzhny Island to probe the mainland coast, previously only explored by RB-47s in operation Home Run. (Map by Tom Cooper based on CIA data)

of this mission are available and almost all mention of it remains redacted from declassified CIA documents.[22]

By the time the U-2s arrived in Norway, the Soviet government had issued notification of closure to shipping for large parts of the Kara and Barents Seas from 20 September through to 25 October 1958. This alerted US agencies to the likely resumption of nuclear tests.[23] There were 15 Soviet air-delivered nuclear tests on Novaya Zemlya between 30 September and 25 October. Thanks to extensive monitoring efforts, the Norwegian and US COMINT ground stations, observed several practice flights before the first live drops and on further occasions during the test period. This established the Soviet's operational pattern and enabled them to pre-warn other agencies of upcoming live explosions. A Soviet Tu-16 Badger would take off from Olenya, on the Kola peninsula, south of Murmansk, approximately two hours before the test to carry out a range reconnaissance mission. It aimed for the radio beacon at Belushya airfield (today identified as Rogachevo) on Novaya Zemlya, then flew over each test drop site before it returned to Olenya via Belushya. For the actual drop, two or three aircraft followed the same route and it was usual for the drop aircraft to make a dummy pass before its actual bomb run.[24] The only real contribution the U-2 could have made to monitoring efforts was to record high altitude fallout drifts, around the test site. A CIA 18 October 1958 notification warned that a 'Soviet picket aircraft' might operate in the area of Novaya Zemlya and instructed the U-2s to maintain high altitude when within 100 miles of its estimated location.[25]

Tamnes indicates that U-2s took off 14–16 times during their deployment, including training and test flights. Technical problems required the replacement of one aircraft.[26] Three U-2s were involved in the deployment: Art 352 (System IV) and 355 were the original deployed aircraft. Art 367 arrived directly from Plattsburgh AB in

New York, flown by Tom Birkhead scheduled for arrival at Bodø on 13 October using the anonymous callsign 'AF3635'.[27] After exchanging ventral hatch covers and drag chutes between the aircraft, 355 was returned to the US.[28]

The subject of some discussion over the years, at least one major penetration mission was planned during this deployment. Some controversy exists as to how much the Norwegians knew in advance of this planned mission. This was later disputed between the two. There were plans for a mission, scheduled for the Polyarny Urals, to be accompanied by a simultaneous System IV mission, numbered 4089 and 4089A respectively. This was cancelled on 19 October. It was then renumbered '4090 & A' (perhaps with some minor route changes) that was itself cancelled on 21 October. It looks as if the two flights then became numbered separately. Penetration Mission 4091 was to be flown on 25 October but is recorded as a weather cancellation. The same day as another, Mission 4092, a 'peripheral ELINT mission' was scheduled to depart Bodø at 0540Z for the estimated 9hrs 25mins flight, which passed North Cape and crossed from the Barents into the Kara Sea flown by Bob Ericson using System IV.[29] He cut short his planned route slightly by going directly from point D to G, as his remaining fuel fell below the projected curve.[30]

Leningrad had been identified as a high priority ELINT target by US Brigadier General Sutterlin, Deputy Director of Operations, in a memo covering 'CHALICE' activities of 9 September 1958. However, there was some reluctance to push ahead with such a mission because of uncertainty over the Soviet response after the Soviets had attacked an RB-47 over the Caspian Sea in July.[31]

There was little point in remaining at Bodø any longer. On 6 November 1958 another ELINT mission was flown from Bodø over the Gulf of Finland and the Baltic Sea, as its return flight to Adana.'

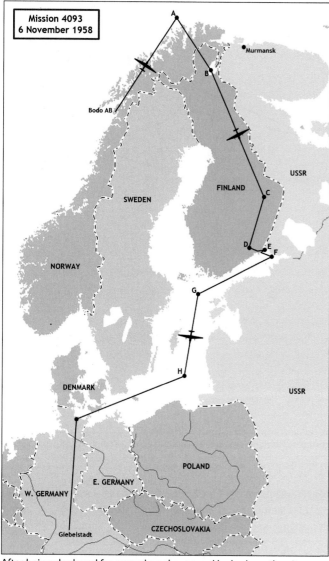

Mission 4093
6 November 1958

After being deployed for several weeks, marred by bad weather, it was decided to return to West Germany. A bold flight, it paralleled the Finnish-Soviet border into the Gulf of Finland, probably with tacit Finnish knowledge. (Map by Tom Cooper based on CIA data)

This was Mission 4093 flown by John Shinn again using 'System IV'. The route has never been officially disclosed, presumably at the behest of the Norwegian and/or Finnish governments. I discovered the proposed route from a record misfiling.

Departing from Bodø, Shinn flew over the sea before turning southwards and paralleled, within around 27–37nm, the Finnish-Soviet border until he entered the Gulf of Finland. It then flew a very short, but demanding navigational leg, down the narrowest part of the Gulf. It flew to within approximately 54nm of Leningrad (St Petersburg) before reversing course. This kept it to within 30km of Finnish soil to the north and the same distance from the Estonian coast to the south. Keeping to the approximate centre of the sea it crossed the Baltic until he turned south over Denmark and returned to Adana. These were the only known missions when System IV was used operationally outside of the Black Sea. There were Soviet attempts to intercept the aircraft which Director Bissell was asked to report on to the White House.[32] Much later Bissell stated that: 'The point of the mission was to stir Russian ELINT along the entire border and make a very sophisticated recording of it, which it succeeded in doing. During that flight, I think we estimated that 57 Russian fighters had been launched against the U-2 at one place or another.'[33]

Although tracked by Soviet radar it was not until 19 January 1959 that the Soviet Foreign Minister delivered a rebuke to the Norwegian Ambassador in Moscow.[34] According to a CIA account, the Norwegian Foreign Ministry was very displeased about not having been internally consulted on the missions, rather than the fact of the flight itself.[35]

In a later letter from Richard Bissell to Colonel Burke, he reflected on some of the shortcomings in the arrangements made for the Bodø based flights. Foremost was that the deployment was arranged undercover as a USAF operation, which at the same time did not follow their normal communication channels with the Norwegians, so attracted their attention.[36] It may also have been the basis for a later observation from Evang: 'It is evident that the Americans, in this case, have only provided the minimum information necessary to obtain clearance. Their initial information was not complete. In any future request for similar operations, we must demand more adequate information. He added, somewhat enigmatically, that the real purpose of the operation had not been achieved, partly due to the weather, but also on account of American political misgivings.'[37] There was no recorded Finnish protest. These were the last U-2 flights involving Norway until the ill-fated Powers mission on 1 May 1960.

Touchdown

Mission 4125 (Touchdown) was the only US U-2 overflight of the USSR in 1959. Piloted by Marty Knutson in Art 367, he took off from Peshawar at 0001Z on 9 July. It was a long-range flight, around 3,300 miles

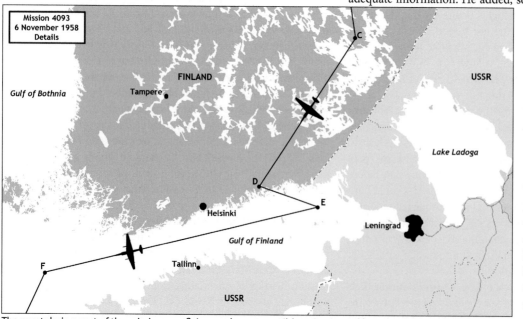

Mission 4093
6 November 1958
Details

The most daring part of the mission was flying as close as possible to Leningrad but remaining in international airspace. The whole mission was subject to multiple intercept efforts by the Soviets. (Map by Tom Cooper based on CIA data)

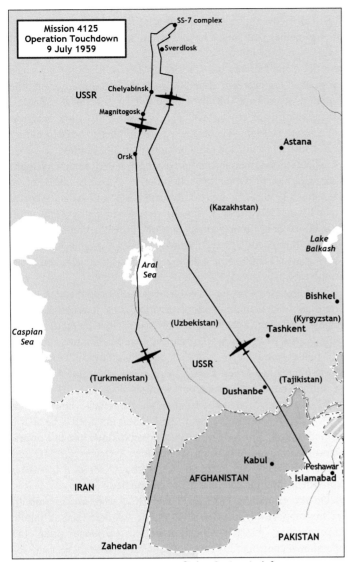

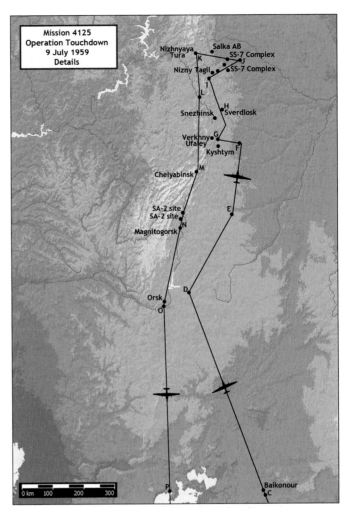

The inset shows the cluster of mainly nuclear-related targets approaching Sverdlovsk that surrounded targets, including research sites, manufacturing centres and an early SS-7 complex, all protected by large numbers of SA-2 SAMs. (Map by Tom Cooper based on CIA data)

By the time of the July 1959 U-2 overflights Soviet air defences were improving greatly, so CHALICE planning staff had to come up with different routes to surprise or outflank them. Touchdown did that by using the isolated Zahedan airfield in Iran as a 'post-strike' staging base. (Map by Tom Cooper based on CIA data)

round trip, northwards deep into the heart of the Soviet Union reaching beyond Sverdlovsk.

Its main targets were nuclear development and research related sites including Kyshtym, Verkhne Nevyansk, Nizhnaya Tura, Kasli. Close to Verkhanya Salda a railway spur was noted under construction, which led to an SS-7 missile complex built shortly afterwards. Subsequent PI reports listed some 53 airfields, including 12 major ones, with 606 aircraft visible. 17 'hexagon' SA-2 SAM sites were identified: Sverdlovsk (seven), Magnitogorsk (two), Chelyabinsk (one), Nizhny Tagil (three), Verkotur'ye (three) and Zlatoust (one). There were 'electronic' sites, and a whole host of mining, chemical and heavy industry plants.[38] Best known publicly from this mission is a single high-quality image of a launchpad at Tyuratam. Imagery of the site revealed considerable extra construction work on launch pads and railway tracks.[39] Another key target included was Vozrozhdeniya Island in the Aral Sea identified as a major biological warfare site (see Chapter 2).

A direct return to Adana was beyond the U-2's range so it had to make a discreet refuelling stop. Marty Knutson landed 9hrs 6mins after take-off and described the event:

The plan called for me to glide over the Urals to save fuel and land at a tiny World War II airstrip near Zahedan, in Iran, right in the triangle where Afghanistan, Iran and Pakistan converge. The Agency would send in a C-130 with agents armed with grenades and Tommy guns to secure the base from mountain bandits who controlled the territory. If I made it across the border and saw a cloud of black smoke, it meant that the field was being attacked by the bandits. If that happened, I was supposed to eject and bailout. I crossed the Russian border with only a hundred gallons remaining. Really getting hairy. I didn't see any smoke, so I came in and landed with less than twenty gallons left in the tank. One of the agents had a six-pack of beer icing. They had an antenna set up and were supposed to send a coded message that I was safe. One of the guys came to me and said, "our equipment is down. I know you're a ham operator, do you, by any chance, know Morse code?" I'm sitting there under a blazing sun, still in my pressure suit, sipping a beer in one hand, and with the other tapping out dots and dashes.[40]

The post-strike C-130 had arrived at Zahedan at 0935Z the day before. It was met by the US Air Attaché from Tehran and had made contact with the airport manager. Parked on a remote part of the field, about one and a half miles from the tower and terminal, an Iranian customs officer made a cursory check of the passenger manifest. Knutson arrived in Art 367 on 9 July at 0907Z. After refuelling and changing the U-2's damaged tail wheel, a replacement ferry pilot took off at 1130Z and headed back to Adana.[41] Senior CIA analyst Dino Brugioni said the mission confirmed to them that the Soviets were not at the time making massive operational missile deployments, but that their 'programmes for research, development and testing were proceeding in an orderly fashion.'[42]

British Deep Penetration Missions

British enthusiasm to participate in overflights saw plans prepared for six missions over the USSR between 1 January and 31 March 1959. This proved to be a wildly over-optimistic programme. The British wanted to mount their flights from Peshawar, believing it offered 'the easiest and best routes to the targets of the highest intelligence value.'[43]

During the planning stage for these missions, Richard Bissell provided what he termed 'technical advice' to Air Marshal Sidney Bufton, the Assistant Chief of the Air Staff for Intelligence. As well as listing five top priority targets, he indicated some additional considerations. First, entering and departing the target airspace via Afghanistan would result in sacrificing some range and key targets. Second, that post-strike staging through Zahedan airfield in Iran would only be justified if the exit from the target area had to be approached through Afghanistan. He indicated his belief that it was 'politically unwise' to suggest the use of Iranian bases. Finally, that: 'exit through Adana [would be] consistent with termination at a British Cyprus base.' He also indicated that whilst concern was growing about the vulnerability of U-2 operations over the USSR that 'Security of movements, penetration times, etc, are the primary concern since premature alert would permit [Soviet] mustering of defence systems.' He also made it very clear that the final choice of overflights must be 'proposed and executed on responsibility and initiative of HMG.' On 10 November 1959, the British Liaison Office in Washington confirmed support from Bissell for the first flight as an ARC 'priority one' mission.[44]

The British Joint Intelligence Committee's (JIC) highest priority targets for this first flight included the bomber plant at Kuybyshev, looking for new bomber types. The Kazan aircraft plant was: 'A most securely guarded bomber production factory about which we have been unable to obtain intelligence.' Planners wanted the flight to follow the railway southwards from Kazan, looking for any spur lines that might be associated with ICBM development – these were the top priority for the US intelligence community – and the major bomber base at Saratov/Engels. Kapustin Yar was a range head that handled all missile research and development. The outbound leg covered the Vozrozhdeniya Island chemical/biological test establishment on the Aral Sea. Following this route was also expected to yield intelligence on a large number of Soviet military and industrial facilities, a flight of more than 3,120 miles.[45]

In late 1959, Macmillan authorised the first RAF Soviet overflight now codenamed Operation High Wire (Mission 8005) on 6 December 1959. With approval from Pakistan's President General Ayub Khan, U-2C Art 351, was ferried to Peshawar by a CIA pilot, with all its identification marks removed. The 'C' model was fitted with the improved Pratt and Whitney J-75-P-13 engine, enabling it to fly above 72,000ft some 4,000ft higher than the U-2A and carry an increased payload of 1,750lb.

'Fast Move' support for this overflight was essential and required almost as much planning and coordination as the main mission. For High Wire this included using C-124C (52-0940 c/s Mast 01), flying from Adana to Peshawar via Bahrein. It pre-positioned the U-2's JP-5 fuel and other supplies. It then flew 990 miles south to Karachi where it remained in case the U-2 became unserviceable and had to be airlifted out. The main support team used C-130A (57-0459 c/s Puffy 02), which landed at Peshawar, via Bahrein, 11 hours before the U-2, to prepare for its arrival. The U-2 was intended to be on the ground at Peshawar for the shortest possible time, just five hours, before departing at 0915Z on its mission. A reserve C-124C and C-130A (56-0539 C/S Puffy 08) were brought forward to Adana from Rhein-Main in case of a major emergency.

On the ground in Pakistan relationships were not so smooth for the support mission. The C-130 pilot was described as 'totally uncooperative,' reluctant to accept he was no longer under the operational control of his parent 322nd Air Division, especially for normal crew rest arrangements. He is recorded as demanding that a motor scooter brought by the Agency support team for local use should be removed. 'He had to be instructed in the fact that he was to fly the aircraft and that it wasn't his responsibility to determine

C-124C 52-0940 was part of the High Wire support operation, able to evacuate the U-2 in case of a major mechanical fault. It is seen here landing at Berlin Tempelhof airport in 1962. (Ralf Manteufel)

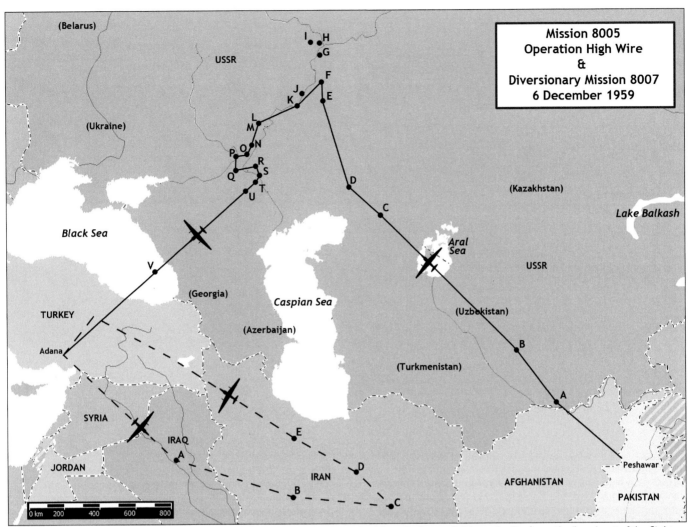

Mission 8005 'High Wire' was the first British-piloted deep penetration. Launched from Peshawar. Robinson had to forgo the 'horn' part of the flight, which would have taken him over the Kazan aircraft plant, due to fuel concerns. A diversionary flight took place way to the south flying over Syria, Iraq and northern Iran. (Map by Tom Cooper based on CIA data)

what gear was, or was not, required for the operation.' CIA staff were also concerned that frequent radio contacts between HQ 322nd AD and the crew might endanger operational security. After it arrived at Peshawar, the C-130A delayed unloading for two hours until the allocated hangar for the operation was cleared of Pakistan AF equipment. The C-124C arrived at Peshawar at 1915Z and the JP-5 fuel drums it carried placed in the hangar awaiting the U-2.[46]

Art 351 arrived at 2305Z. It was taken into the hangar and immediately prepared for the mission flight. Meanwhile, Robbie Robinson (and the reserve pilot) were given a final briefing at 2215Z and had 'ample time' to study the final route. Robinson elected not to carry his 'lethal pill' on the mission. The CIA after action report described it as 'too dangerous and fragile to carry on the aircraft without special safeguards. The device is also too large to conceal on the person.' Both pilots commenced pre-breathing oxygen from 0200Z. Robinson boarded his U-2 an hour before launch, whilst it was still in the hangar. It was towed out to the runway for launch. It had been on the ground for a fraction under five hours and departed at 0400Z on 6 December 1959.[47] For Mission 8005 Robinson took off from Peshawar and headed northwest to cross the Soviet border from Afghanistan, where Soviet radar coverage was assessed as weakest, for his 8hr 30min mission.[48] For the first 700 miles, the ground was not visible due to undercast. Using dead reckoning navigation he accumulated a 40-mile error which he corrected by the time he passed point Echo. Contrails ceased at the expected 55,000ft but as he approached his first target at 70,000ft, occasional

light trails with larger 'puffs' appeared so Robinson climbed slightly to clear them, but this was not totally effective, still with occasional short trails. At point Sierra, Robinson descended to 70,000ft again.[49]

Robinson had explained some of the handling characteristics for the U-2 in his 1993 interview with Paul Lashmar:

For a jet, it was unusual, as you landed like a taildragger – tail down. It was heavy on the controls when flying, but came into its own at higher altitudes – it was happier the higher it got. The real problem was it would never have been accepted into British service, as it would not have passed testing at Boscombe Down because it was structurally unsound. To fly at those high altitudes, it had to be light, therefore it was structurally weak. It was the only aeroplane I have flown that if you were ham-fisted with the controls, you could have destroyed it. If you pulled back on the stick too hard the tail could fall off. When flying it, you were aware it was a very fragile machine.

It was an aircraft you had to treat with considerable respect, with its very limited never-to-exceed velocity. We climbed steeply on take-off so as not to [go above] the limiting speed. The U-2 at 70,000ft flew as most aircraft do at 35,000ft. It was happy at very high altitudes where the stresses were lower.[50]

The U-2s never to exceed velocity was Mach 0.8. Its notorious 'coffin corner' issues meant at its highest altitudes flying just two

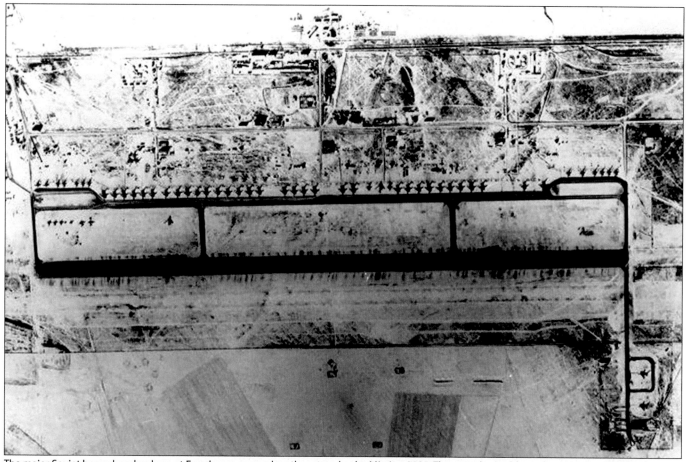

The major Soviet heavy bomber base at Engels was covered on the return leg by Mission 8005. The very clear cold weather that day produced exceptionally high-quality imagery that allowed positive identification of individual aircraft types. However, this released image appears to be significantly degraded to hide its true quality in comparison to the Vlaidimorvka airfield photograph. (CIA)

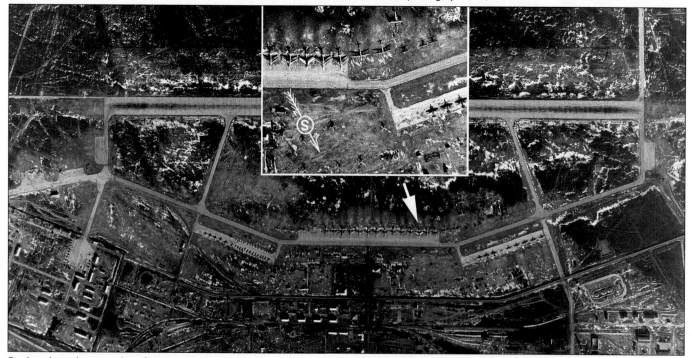

Further along the return leg of Mission 8005, Robbie Robinson captured Vlaidimorvka airfield (Akhtubinsk). This shot shows some of the 216 aircraft present and identified in the Mission Coverage Plot. (NARA, courtesy Chris Pocock)

knots above Mach 0.8 could result in airframe over stressing and structural damage and three knots below possibly entering a stall.

'During these overflights, we carried the B camera, which filled the entire equipment bay. We also carried ELINT recorders.' During the flight, Robinson became concerned about his U-2's higher-than-expected fuel use, caused by stronger than forecast high altitude winds and his higher cruise altitude than originally anticipated. Built into the mission plan were two 'cut off' points to shorten his route if fuel consumption was excessive. At the first point, Robinson's remaining fuel was 30 gallons below that required for completion of the mission so he opted to forgo the Kazan aircraft plant thus shortening his route. For the last 1,000 miles of his flight, including his exit over the USSR, undercast again prevented further photography.[51] He arrived back at Adana having been airborne for 8hrs 15mins.

As Robinson was heading towards his targets, Flt Lt Michael Bradley mounted a diversionary mission (8007B) well to the south. He had taken off from Adana at 1040L, turned southeast over Syria before heading east across southern Iraq and on to Isfahan in central Iran. Approaching the Afghan border, he reversed course to head roughly north-westerly. Passing over Tehran, he made for Sivas in central Turkey, where he turned south and recovered to Adana at 1700hrs – 2hrs 30mins after Robinson had landed. Bradley's aircraft had carried System IV equipment, but unfortunately, the 14-track recorder had malfunctioned just 20 minutes into the flight.

Exceptional weather conditions during Robinson's mission, with dense very cold clear air, enabled exceptionally high-quality photography for much of his flight. Within 12 hours of the film arriving at Adana, it was on its way to Rhein-Main and then Washington DC for full exploitation. The exposed film was processed by Eastman Kodak in Rochester, New York. Robinson explained: 'One [tracker] camera was on the whole time from take-off to landing.' That film was processed at Adana with copies forwarded to London and Washington.[52] Quick examination soon revealed High Wire had detected 15 Tu-95 Bear and 23 Tu-16 Badger bombers at Kuybyshev-Bezymyanka and 37 Myasishchev M-4 Bisons, 20 Badgers, 44 various fixed-wing aircraft and 38 assorted helicopters at Engels. Robinson said he was surprised by 'The number of chemical and biological production plants' that the Soviets had constructed. And added that British pilots: 'were shown lots of the [mission] pictures by our representatives – much more than the American crews were.' From that collected imagery, draughtsmen produced very detailed drawings of the target sites showing the various individual buildings and their dimensions.

Knife Edge Flight

The second British overflight mission was codenamed Knife Edge. Provisionally scheduled for 13 January 1960, it was repeatedly delayed because of unsatisfactory weather over the target areas. Designated Mission 8009, John McArthur finally took off from Peshawar on February 5.

Concerns about numerous highly defended areas along the planned route meant McArthur remained above 70,000ft throughout the mission. Given the extreme distances involved, Merzifon airfield in Turkey's Black Sea region was designated as the emergency fuel diversion if required. To ensure the British pilots were suitably prepared, they had practised 'let downs' and approach procedures there using a T-33 before the mission. With approval from Pakistan's president, a Fast Move C-130 (c/s Wiley 04) arrived at Peshawar, with a C-124 (c/s Mast 97) again positioned at Karachi.[53]

Mission 8009 Intelligence Report

A more detailed analysis of the publicly available data relating to Mission 8009 is useful. Although the nature of this mission has been well known for some time, it was only in 2019 that the MoD finally allowed public access to the detailed mission files. They provide another source against which to validate the US data already released. Primarily a British mission, it illustrates their high level of integration into this US operation. The main targets came from a British JIC list compiled in conjunction with James Reber's ARC. British interests remained focussed on the bomber airfields – especially the Kazan area – that Robinson was unable to image.

The mission intelligence report stated that over Kazan: 'Seven bombers of a new type, resembling the Backfin were identified' – these were most likely early Tu-22 Blinders. Flt Lt David Dowling mounted a diversionary flight, designated 8010. It again carried the often-problematic Haller-Raymond-Brown System IV. Flying further south this time, Dowling broadly paralleled the Iranian-Soviet border fully aware that 'enemy' radar could likely detect aircraft as far south as Tehran. His onboard receivers functioned successfully – although most experienced significant noise levels from the U-2's own electrical systems. Plans called for the 'diversionary' flight to take place after the main mission aircraft had cleared Soviet airspace, to avoid alerting air defences to an ongoing overflight.[55] There is a close comparison between British and US data for the mission.

Table 5: Mission 8009, 'Knife Edge'[3]	
No. of locations	Target typology
75	Airfields: major fighter, bomber bases, grass fields, abandoned.
20	Unidentified airfields: unnamed, mostly grass, abandoned or under construction.
42	Telecommunication sites: microwave stations, radar sites, comm masts, radio and TV stations, DF stations, 'electronics sites.'
80	Industry: oil refinery, oil field, rubber products, heavy equipment, chemical, aircraft engine, airframe assembly, optical, agricultural, iron, steel, power plants, substations, chemical, vehicle, dam, drilling installations, mining, machine tools and unidentified.
57	Military Installations: ammunition depots, barracks, vehicle parks, aircraft maintenance, training installations, firing ranges, explosives plant anti-aircraft, repair facilities, coastal defences, artillery and equipment parks.
24	SAM sites: SAM bases, support facilities, support facilities.
11	Naval installations: military docks, submarine and naval bases, shipyards, Naval HQs, naval weapons' storage.
22	Ports & harbours: River and Black Sea port facilities.
61	Storage: petrol & oil, explosives, unidentified.
35	Transportation: bridges, rail stations, repair yards, marshalling yards, pipelines, vehicle depots.
118	Urban areas: cities and towns.
26	Miscellaneous: unidentified buildings and installations.
571	Total
3. Joint Mission Coverage B8009, 5 February 1960, (CIA-RDP90B00224R000300380005-6).	

MISSION 8009 'KNIFE EDGE'

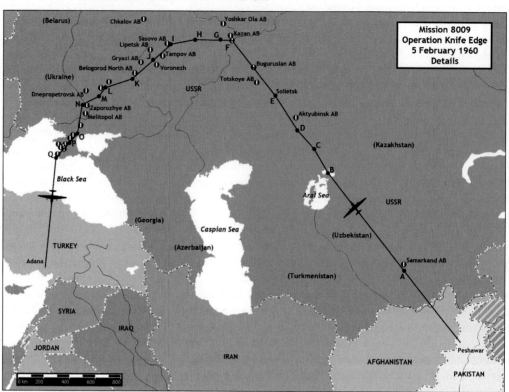

From the flight's route we can see, as might be expected, that as McArthur flew northwards over today's Uzbekistan there was little of military interest. It was only as the mission passed Aktyubinsk, 1,250nm from Peshawar, that the target density increases. As the flight approached Kazan and turned west, target numbers increased significantly.

The images only highlight 45 airfields because identifying the other 526 targets along the entire flight route, against modern-day imagery is now a near-impossible task. Many have long since been abandoned or converted to alternative uses. The flight covered more than 3,000 miles.

An overview of Mission 8009's route and some of the airfields imaged along it. These are not all of them, just those still identifiable from modern imagery. Since 1960 many have been abandoned and some subsequently built over, but even so, this amounted to some 45 of the 75 identified locations in the Mission Coverage Summary for 8009.[54] There are differences in precise longitude and latitude locations between 1950s era charts and modern-day satellite imagery. (Map by Tom Cooper based on Landsat/Copernicus, SIO, NOAA, USN, GEBCO, IBCAO, Geo-Base DE, SK Telecom)

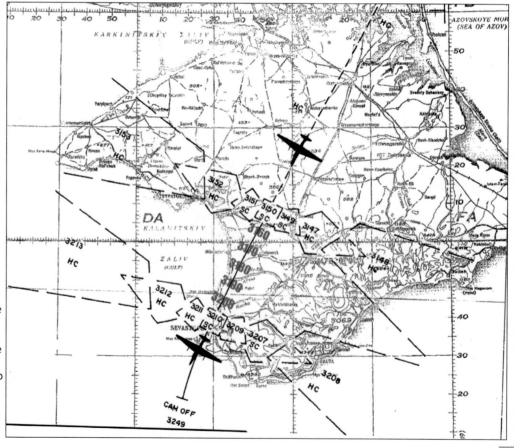

An extract of the Knife Edge Mission Plot where the PIs plotted the U-2's course over the Crimea. On the map, for clarity's sake, the footprint of the seven B camera image group that gave lateral coverage in Mode 1 were marked. That enabled analysts to be more selective in the images they later requested as prints to examine in later analysis. (CIA/Kevin Wright)

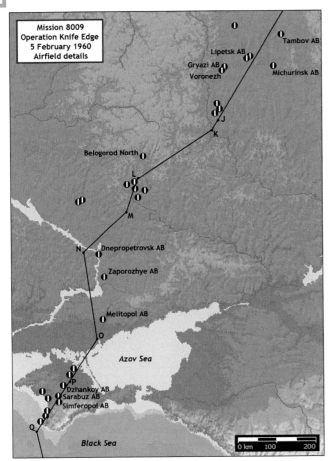

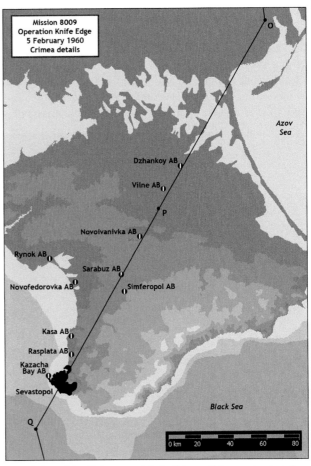

By far the highest concentration of imaged airfields were on the south-westerly leg of the flight, especially in Crimea. This was also true for most other types of military installation. It proved impossible to locate on modern imagery clear evidence of SAM related sites. (Map by Tom Cooper based on Landsat/Copernicus, SIO, NOAA, USN, GEBCO, IBCAO, Geo-Base DE, SK Telecom)

This image shows part of the Kazan aircraft plant site, the key assembly plant. The aircraft patterns in the snow in the bottom right-hand corner of the image resemble the shape of Tu-22 Blinders. (NARA, courtesy Chris Pocock).

ARZAMAS–16

Carefully omitted from the Mission Coverage Plot, still redacted today, are any references to nuclear-related installations. McArthur's course (between point H and I) took him within 12 miles of Arzamas-16, the site was named by PIs. Really Sarov, it is 75 miles from the town of Arzamas, 240nm from Moscow. It houses a major nuclear weapon warhead assembly/disassembly plant and the research institute that was a major photographic coup for Mission 8009. One released image has been identified from Mission 8009, which covers what appears to be part of the research site. Even from that one image, cloud excepting, McArthur must have captured additional useable shots of Arzamas-16. Up until 1967, it was protected by an SA-2 SAM site.

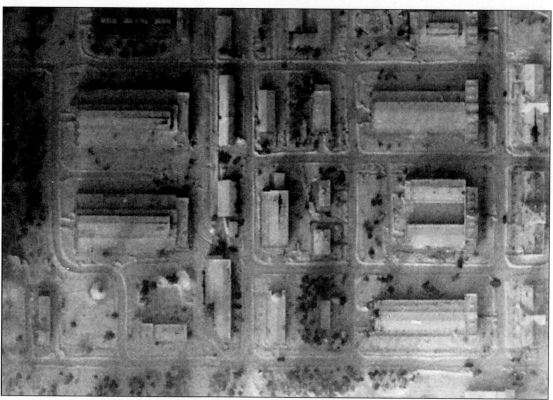

Original image from Mission 8009 of nuclear research institute as Arzamas–16. (CIA)

A comparative image from today of 8009's research institute, shows very little has changed. (Maxar Tech, Landsat/COPERNICUS, CNES/Airbus)

The roughly 100-square mile area today remains bounded by a double fence. There are only two entrances to the city that houses over 95,000 people – about 20,000 work in the design institute and another 10,000 at the warhead plant. It has been compared to Los Alamos in the US. Within the city – which has its own airfield – there is major recent development.[56]

The closed city of Sarov today, with the original 8009 area image labelled. The whole city is fenced in with limited manned check-point entrances. It continues to be a major nuclear site, with the city served by its own airfield. (Maxar Tech, Landsat/COPERNICUS, CNES/Airbus)

Original 8009 image showing nuclear weapon 'Explosive test cell' at Arzamas–16. (CIA)

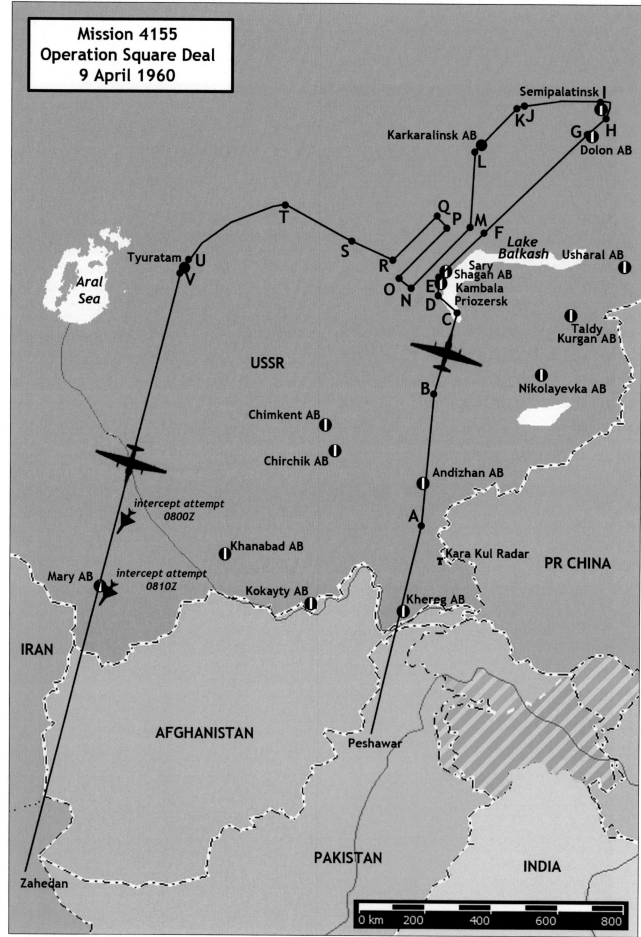

**Mission 4155
Operation Square Deal
9 April 1960**

Semipalatinsk

K J

Karkaralinsk AB

G H

Dolon AB

L

Q

P

M

F

Lake Balkash

Usharal AB

T

S

R

Sary Shagan AB

Kambala

O

E

Kama

N

D

Priozersk

C

Taldy Kurgan AB

Tyuratam U

V

Aral Sea

B

Nikolayevka AB

USSR

Chimkent AB

Chirchik AB

Andizhan AB

A

intercept attempt 0800Z

Khanabad AB

Kara Kul Radar

PR CHINA

Mary AB

intercept attempt 0810Z

Kokayty AB

Khereg AB

IRAN

AFGHANISTAN

Peshawar

PAKISTAN

INDIA

0 km   200   400   600   800

Zahedan

Mission 4155 flew a search pattern north of Lake Balkash in the hope of finding signs of an ICBM complex. That added considerably to its vulnerability with attempts to intercept it as it exited towards Iran. (Map by Tom Cooper based on Landsat/Copernicus, SIO, NGA, USN, GEBCO)

Square Deal

The final successful overflight of the Soviet Union took place on 9 April 1960 and was codenamed Square Deal, Mission 4155: it was planned as one of the six original British missions. This longer flight had the added complication that a necessary refuelling stop required the use of Zahedan again, close to the Iranian-Afghanistan border before the U-2 could fly onto Adana. Although it appears to have been planned as a British flight, it switched at a very late date to a US primary pilot.

This mission planning indicates just how integrated US and British missions were. British proposals for the route were first circulated to the OLDSTER unit on 6 January 1960. By 27 January 1960, the main route had been revised after consultation with the ARC, the British JIC and the CHALICE team. It continued to be updated until the last moment as the British route came to resemble much more closely that generated by the Americans.[57] The British proposal did not include the Tyuratam launch site, but this was later added by the Americans so including a high priority target without requiring a major route change. The 'search pattern' flown northeast of Lake Balkalsh was intended to bisect any railway lines in the hope of finding test, or potentially operational, ICBM sites. It added considerable mission time and increased the U-2's exposure to Soviet interception, which indicates the intelligence priority accorded to the task. The city of Karkalinsk was added at a late stage by the ARC, via the British Representation in Washington DC.

The use of Zahedan was arranged by the US Air Force on the 'basis that this is a normal refuelling stop in connection with a meteorological flight in the Middle East.'[58] There was some discussion about the level at which the approach be made to the Iranians, in the wake of the July 1959 Touchdown mission, that had apparently rankled with some of the military. Colonel Horras, the US Air Attaché in Tehran, reported he had met with the Iranian intelligence chief and was told of their unhappiness with that operation in 'That the actions of the personnel involved were not consistent with an open and above-board operation and that a mysterious plane arrived in Zahedan and departed Zahedan without proper clearances.' Colonel Horras suggested that a direct approach to the Shah, to gain his approval, would carry the necessary weight to overcome any Iranian military objections.[59] Oil was soon poured on troubled waters when US State Department further investigations revealed why the Touchdown mission C-130 had not 'behaved normally.' An onboard radio failure was blamed for its failure to contact Tehran or Zahedan air traffic and so had arrived partially unexpectedly. Horras was assured that no approach to the Shah was necessary and the Iranian Chief of Staff was satisfied that the existing: 'Blanket refuel clearance for support aircraft and "single-engine jet" aircraft remains in force.'[60] Afterwards, the Americans went to considerable effort to ensure they adhered to the agreed flight plans and kept the Iranians updated with the many changes to support aircraft allocations that occurred.

The support operation was again considerable. It involved three C-130s using the RAF airfield at Bahrein and cover name 'Exercise Landlubber' beginning on 7 April 1960. From there C-130A 55-0014 (c/s Puffy 62) moved onto Peshawar. 55-50020 (c/s Wiley 90) proceeded to Peshawar then after unloading retired to Karachi. C-130A 55-0011 (c/s Lager 95/Puffy 16) went on to Zahedan.[61]

It was only on 6 April, three days before the mission, there was confirmation of the swap to a CIA pilot instead of a British one.[62] The sudden switch appears related to a change in US priorities. During the planning period since January 1960, Square Deal was the third choice of mission because two others, Time Step and Grand Slam, were considered a higher priority. Suddenly the intended Norwegian launch base/destination for these missions became unavailable (understood to be Bodø) due to it: 'being utilised in NATO exercises… [REDACTED] and therefore impractical for use from a security standpoint during the period.'[63] Square Deal now became the priority for the US and with political authority already granted by Eisenhower, they took over the mission lead.

Art 344 was selected as the diversionary aircraft (for mission 4157) but was swapped for 355 at the last moment because of a maintenance issue, so took off 20 minutes late at 0221Z flown by Jim Barnes. It carried only a tracker camera for its flight. Art 351 was the main mission aircraft and flown by Bob Ericson (Gary Powers was the backup) and lifted off from Peshawar on 9 April 1960 at 0055Z. It was just one day before the deadline Eisenhower had given for completing the mission.

The flight was successful, although substantial portions of the route were covered by cloud. It covered many locations related to Soviet missile testing and development. This included some of the development work that was ongoing at Sary Shagan, on the edge of Lake Balkalsh, up to the edge of the Semipalatinsk nuclear test ground and on the exit leg from the Tyuratam launch centre. The search pattern flown to the north-west of Lake Balkalsh was a risky move. Flying such a near repetitive pattern allowed the Russians an opportunity to better coordinate their air defence effort, no matter its limited effectiveness. Flying the search pattern further limited the U-2's possible exit routes to a safe destination. This probably accounts for the greater success of interception efforts reported on the exit leg. KWCROWN-6 (ACAS (I) AVM Sidney Bufton) said he believed: 'That successful avoidance of detection in recent missions [was] probably due to [Soviet] belief that straight tracks were friendly but on 4155 backtracking may have attracted attention and raised suspicion.' In a later message, he further explained that for those reasons he had always been opposed to such a search pattern. However, in the end, the search for such high priority, but unknown targets, the intelligence need had outweighed operational considerations.[64]

Ericson's aircraft was soon detected and tracked by Soviet radars in southern Turkmenistan. Several efforts to intercept it early on were unsuccessful. Later, in a final desperate attempt, two MiG-19s were launched from Merv (Mary) airbase, almost directly overflown by Ericson. Two pilots were ordered to pursue the U-2 over Iran and intercept it as it started to descend, but both returned to base, probably due to fuel shortage. Unfortunately, one of the pilots, Senior Lt Vladimir Karcheveski, was killed in a crash recovering to his base.[65]

Once Square Deal was completed attention quickly switched to the next mission. Two were in prospect: Time Step and Grand Slam. Whilst the intelligence picture was still far from complete, U-2 missions had revealed a lot more about the southern USSR than was available when they started overflights, just four years previously. The same was not true for the north-western Soviet Union.

The U-2's performance had improved significantly since 1956. Especially following the introduction of the U-2C. Now it could fly further, higher and carry a bigger payload. But there were penalties. Flying higher made the aircraft safer from Soviet air defences, but reduced its range, even with the addition of wing-mounted slipper tanks, now regularly carried. Not only were the capabilities of Soviet air defences improving, through fighters and SA-2 sites, but with only a limited number of entry and exit points along the southern Soviet frontier, made it easier for the defences to pre-plan their responses to U-2 penetrations. The deeper they flew into the

USSR, from Pakistan, the fewer were the exit options available. The cumulative effects of these factors were shortening the odds-on a U-2 overflight being brought down.

For a while, a mission codenamed Time Step was considered. This would have taken off from Thule in Greenland, flown along the northern coast of the USSR before passing over Novaya Zemlya. Heading inland it would have covered Pletesk and Severodvinsk then turned north again to cover Murmansk before landing in Norway.[66] Sun Spot was a third priority mission considered. That would have departed Peshawar, covered Tyuratam, Vladimirovka, production facilities at Dnepropetrovsk and Kyiv, plus five long-range bomber bases, before recovering to Adana.[67]

Further, operations from Scandinavia were problematic. Sweden was impossible. Finnish airspace had been penetrated a few times, probably at least with their tacit connivance, but to do so too often would risk Soviet threats and hurt the Finnish government. Norway was the best bet, but they were under significant Russian pressure too. Few within Norway's government knew details of its involvement. Had it been public knowledge there almost certainly would have been domestic political consequences. Without a Scandinavian airfield being available missions over the Murmansk peninsula, Pletesk and other vital areas of interest were all but impossible. Thule might have been possible for occasional missions but generally conditions there were not regularly suitable.

A north to south or south to north route across the whole USSR became the most likely to succeed. It would break the pattern of recent missions since the Soft Touch series, of departures from Pakistan. But to follow such a plan brought the U-2 to the limits of its range and left little margin for error. It would involve flying long straight legs to cover the necessary distances, with little room for serious feints to try and fool Soviet defences.

Grand Slam

Grand Slam was the second choice of three possible missions that pushed right up to the 1 May 1960 deadline imposed by President Eisenhower before the summit conference in Geneva. Using Fast Move staging arrangements, Grand Slam was mounted from Peshawar in Pakistan. After a late switch in aircraft, Powers took off at 0159Z in Art 360. He headed deep into the USSR, on the U-2's twenty-fourth deep penetration overflight of Soviet territory. As he approached the Sverdlovsk Oblast, he was 800 miles east of Moscow. From there he would have exited Soviet territory via the high priority target area around Murmansk, headed for Bodø in Norway. Four hours into his mission his aircraft was struck by an SA-2.

Nearly two years later on February 10, 1962, Powers walked across the Glienicke Bridge in Berlin, exchanged for Soviet spy Colonel Rudolph Abel. Just three days later, on 13 February he began his

debrief with senior CIA personnel. The transcripts from those debriefing sessions, conducted over several days, make fascinating reading. Powers' recollections of the preparations for the mission and the flight itself are particularly interesting. He discussed the late exchange of his original aircraft and its replacement with Art 360. Powers was given some special instructions relating to this aircraft as it had previously experienced fuel feed problems. Indeed, it had run out of fuel and had force landed at Fukisawa Airport, close to Astugi AB (see Volume 2). Det B commander Colonel Shelton had briefed him on the arrangements in case he ran short, or out, of fuel as he approached the end of his mission passing over Scandinavia. This included marking possible emergency landing airfields on his map.

In the cockpit at Peshawar, Powers' departure was delayed by some 30 minutes due to poor communications. Bob Ericson, the reserve pilot for the mission assisted Powers with his final departure preparations. During that delay Ericson had taken off his shirt to shade Powers to help reduce his discomfort from the rapidly increasing temperatures until he received the final 'Go.' When Ericson saw the launch signal from the tower, he patted Powers on the back and said 'good luck.' He stepped back and within six minutes Powers said he was airborne. He soon encountered heavy overcast that complicated navigation. However, radio fixes helped him maintain a roughly accurate course. His first target was just south of the Aral Sea, where the cloud briefly broke and enabled some visual navigation. Establishing he was 20-30 miles east of his planned course Powers began course correction.

He soon noticed contrails off to the right, well below him, each heading in opposite directions which he assumed to be fighters searching for him. Unable to see the ground again, and the late departure having upset his pre-computed sextant settings, he could not determine his exact position. However, he continued heading for Sverdlovsk. Just south of Chelyabinsk the autopilot started to give him problems, a continuous headache for all U-2 pilots. Disconnecting it he flew the aircraft manually, before reconnecting the autopilot and which he very soon had to disconnect again. To the south of Sverdlovsk and heading roughly north-westerly, he says

On 10 February 1962 Gary Powers was exchanged for Colonel Rudolf Abel on the Glienicke Bridge in Berlin. After debriefing by the CIA he was called to appear before the Senate Armed Services Committee on 6 March 1962. (Library of Congress)

he passed over an unidentified airfield (Koltsovo airport). It was then that his aircraft was hit. As he recounted during his debrief:

> I was lined up perfectly on this flight line – everything was fine, I just rolled on my turn and got lined up taking some interim instrument readings and recording oxygen, normal procedure, when I felt or heard an explosion … I don't know whether I heard it or not, but I felt it – just like everything stopped, and I can't say that I heard it – I don't know … I immediately looked up and all I could see through my canopy was just orange light, everything I could see was that colour.
>
> This explosion seemed to be behind me and to the right. I was looking at the instruments at the time. I had just looked at them, everything was perfect. The only thing wrong with the aircraft was the autopilot pitch control and I wasn't using the autopilot. I remember saying to myself, or saying out loud, I think it was 'Oh, God, I've had it now,' or something like that, the first thing that entered my mind. I couldn't tell you how much time passed, it just seemed that everything was standing still for a little while. I just saw that red glow, looked down. The right-wing started to drop. I corrected it and brought the right-wing up fine. The nose started to drop and I pulled back on the stick and there was no connection between the controls and the tail. The plane just nosed straight over and I feel sure that the wings broke off, they must have folded down and come off. The airplane tumbled on over, ended up in an inverted position nose high…[68]

Powers battled for some time to get out of his stricken aircraft and eventually freed himself. His parachute automatically opened and he landed in a field near a tractor, missing nearby power lines. He was quickly helped by the locals. It was not long before he was passed up the chain of command and taken to Moscow for detailed interrogation and ultimately his show trial in July 1960.[69] There he received a 10-year sentence at what became a worldwide media event.

Following his exchange, the CIA debrief was naturally extensive. He was asked lots of questions about events on the day he was shot down and the self-destruct charge on the aircraft and his lethal injection pin. Before take-off, the pin had been taken out of the hollow coin (intended to disguise it) and placed in a pocket of his flight suit. He was questioned about the way the Soviets treated him, what he might have seen whilst imprisoned, the questions his Soviet interrogators posed, especially those surrounding Adana and US activities there.[70]

One more trivial point discussed, was a statement by one of Powers' debriefers. He indicated that the Agency had regularly painted numbers on the U-2 and removed them again and asked Powers if the issue was ever raised with him by his Soviet interrogators. They had indeed done so on several occasions to which Powers said he did not know about. He believed the Russians had removed paint off some of the wreckage, looking for 'numbers and insignias and so forth.'[71]

What comes across from all the debrief transcripts is Powers' great dignity and the sheer common sense he applied to his time in Soviet custody. He maintained that his Soviet captors had treated him reasonably well, nor was he tortured. He says his interrogators did not always pursue his responses, largely accepting what he told them. Powers said from conversations with unit Security Officers and others at Adana, during his time flying U-2s, he adopted the position that if he was captured deep inside the Soviet Union he might as well tell the basic truth. The Soviets could have discovered

much of it themselves anyway. He reasoned that by being essentially truthful about such things it would perhaps enable him to sidestep other, more sensitive subjects. One such topic he 'protected' from his interrogators was Detachment B's wide-ranging U-2 Middle East flight programme. The Soviet intelligence officers appeared to know nothing of that activity and did not raise any questions about it with him.[72] His approach appears to have been largely successful. It also seemed to confound his Agency debriefers, who spent considerable time trying to ascertain who told Powers to behave the way he did if captured, and when.[73] Such an experienced U-2 pilot as Powers knew a great deal about many aspects of the U-2 programme and could have revealed to his interrogators much more. He essentially stuck to the line that he was just a 'driver' and did not know much else about what went on at Adana. He could do that successfully because his basic story was essentially accurate and the interrogators could not fault it. Probably unknown to him, it also played into the Soviet model of the way they trained and treated their armed forces, revealing to individuals only the minimum of information needed to do their job. As a result, they perhaps more readily accepted what Powers said as 'normal.'

The embarrassment of Powers' show trial was followed by greatly increased congressional interest and stronger oversight in Washington. Imprisoned, Powers' had undoubtedly suffered personally. After his release, Powers appeared before the Senate Armed Services Committee to be further questioned. Whilst many intelligence professionals had quietly praised him, there was a great deal of unfounded widespread public, media and political criticism directed at him. There were even calls from some for him to be tried for treason because he had not killed himself and instead allowed himself to be taken prisoner. Others accused him of revealing all the U-2's secrets to the Soviets. This was a huge injustice for one of the CIA's most experienced and professional pilots.

Grand Slam hindsight

The great benefit of hindsight points to several key factors behind the loss of Grand Slam. The Soviets had become used to U-2 missions launched from Pakistan. Their southern air defences had been considerably strengthened with better radar coverage, more fighters and large numbers of SA-2s. The air defences became more proficient as the different elements were better integrated.

The deepest missions over the USSR, like Grand Slam, limited possible exit routes to safe landing grounds. However, it was perhaps the day selected for Powers to fly his mission that was the single biggest factor that made his tracking and eventual loss most likely, coupled with a bit of Soviet luck. May Day, one of the most important public holidays of the Soviet year, could have been a day when Soviet defences were at their most relaxed. Indeed, there were very few aircraft aloft over the entire USSR, so when Powers' U-2 appeared on their radar screens and was intermittently tracked, it was easier to classify the contact as a US overflight. The lack of air traffic meant he was not able to 'disappear' amongst the much larger volumes usually present on any usual working day and that would normally have made him much more difficult to track. By the time he approached the strategically important city of Sverdlovsk, Soviet air defences were at high readiness.

Colonel Don Emmons, a USAF SR-71 RSO, was a long-time friend of Marty Knutson. He relayed to me a story Knutson later told him about that day. Waiting at Bodø with the staging team for Powers to arrive, he was already pre-breathing oxygen. The plan was to refuel and relaunch the U-2 on to Turkey as soon as possible with Marty as the ferry pilot. As Powers became significantly overdue, Knutson waited suited and pre-breathing oxygen. Over five hours later, Knutson was well aware that Powers would not arrive. Sometime after that, via HBJAYWALK, they were told to evacuate from Bodø as quickly as possible. The team rapidly packed up the equipment and the crew started the C-130. One engine failed to start, so the Air Force pilot began to power down the Hercules intending to await a repair. At that stage, Knutson told the C-130 captain, in forcible terms, that they were working for the CIA now, not the Air Force and they were to get going and take-off from Bodø as quickly as possible, three engines or not, which they did.[74]

The loss brought an abrupt halt to U-2 overflight missions of the USSR. All CIA U-2 missions halted and the British contingent was immediately withdrawn from Turkey, according to a prearranged emergency evacuation plan. Following the loss, there were major political ramifications. Initially, there was complete political embarrassment because the Americans' original cover story was publicly shown to be a complete lie by Khruschev and with a living pilot its prisoner. It brought detailed worldwide media exposure to the US overflight programme. It became immediately clear that Eisenhower was very deeply involved in its conduct. There were Soviet protests to Pakistan and Norway, followed by major recriminations over their role in facilitating the missions.

The loss of a U-2 had long been predicted. The Agency itself had expected it might be able to get away with Soviet overflights into late 1957 but managed up to 1960, when an SA-2 had, unrealised at the time, brought down a U-2 over China, a short time before Powers. The concerns about the SA-2's capabilities were already a major focus of dedicated western intelligence collection efforts, that continued into the late 1970s.

The loss of Gary Powers brought an immediate halt not only to the overflights but also caused a significant pause to the many other US peripheral and electronic reconnaissance operations. It brought an end to all major US overflights of the USSR and East European satellites. But what about other countries? The Peoples Republic of China was of growing in strategic interest. Then there were the many hot spots that periodically erupted across the world, especially in the Middle East and the Pacific region. Basing agreements with foreign governments to allow reconnaissance operations from their territory came under increased scrutiny and greater formalisation. A significantly new pattern of arrangements emerged by September 1960, which endured to the end of the Cold War and beyond. Of even greater long-term significance was the first successful recovery of a film 'bucket' from a Corona satellite in August 1960. Whilst that imagery covered much bigger areas than the U-2 fleet could, its original quality was considerably inferior. Over the next few years, it improved greatly but until that time the U-2 still had valuable tasks to perform. Their next great adventure would be centred on bases in east Asia, especially Taiwan and Thailand.

6
MANAGING THE 'TAKE'

If planning and flying U-2 missions was a major accomplishment, dealing with what it brought home was no small achievement either. As U-2 operations spread worldwide so too were the efforts necessary to collect the exposed film and SIGINT tapes, process and analyse them.

Before the first U-2 missions the amount of overhead imagery collected from covert US penetration and peripheral flights was small and managed by a cell within the Pentagon. Even for important targets it usually amounted to just a handful of photographs. Those first U-2 missions alone generated thousands of images each and

changed the handling of photographic intelligence forever. In way of loose description in just four years from July 1956 to August 1960, the CIA's own figures indicated that its U-2s produced some 25 miles of 70mm 'tracker' film and the equivalent to 220 miles of nine-inch wide 'basic intelligence film.' As collection activities multiplied, especially after the arrival of Corona satellite imagery in August 1960, the amount of imagery massively expanded.

The north-eastern US, especially around Boston, Massachusetts, became a key location for covert US photographic reconnaissance support activities. Optical research was spearheaded from Boston University and its Optical Research Laboratory (BUORL). Lens designer James Baker was at Harvard, companies like ITEK and Perkin-Elmer – initially closely associated with the research work – set up in the area. Eastman Kodak in NY and its Air Force counterpart, responsible for much of the photographic film development and subsequent processing. All were relatively close to Washington DC with the Federal government, intelligence agencies and Pentagon within a few hours' drive.

The Lincoln Plant in Rochester, NY was the location for processing early U-2 imagery. (CSNR/Alkins)

Kodak's Hawkeye plant, also in Rochester NY, was a much more modern facility, with more space, to process U-2 and satellite imagery. (CSNR/ R and J Sherwood)

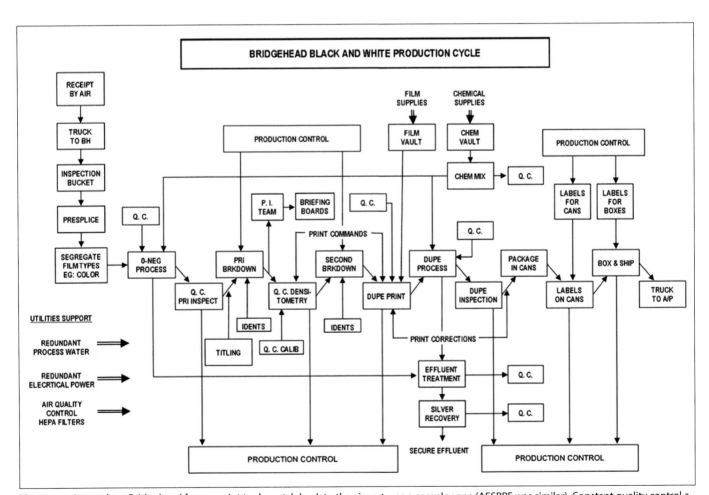

The processing cycle at Bridgehead from receipt to despatch back to the airport was a complex one (AFSPPF was similar). Constant quality control a necessity throughout the entire cycle. (CSNR, *Bridgehead*, p.133)

During 1955 preparations began for the expected imminent arrival of U-2 imagery, concentrated on handling, processing and disseminating finished materials. It became the territory of institution-building and bureaucratic empires. But initially at least, what needed to be done was quite clear. Once the exposed material reached the continental US the first stage was to process it.

Bridgehead

Eastman Kodak, at Rochester NY, played a leading role in the development of the highly specialised film payloads carried by reconnaissance aircraft and later satellite programmes. It designed, built and utilised much of the highly specialised equipment necessary to handle, process and print U-2 material. The company was selected for the task by the CIA as the complexity of the work was believed to be beyond the technical skills available within government at the time. The Land Panel members supported the CIA's approach to the company and a formal contract was signed on 1 October 1955 for the operation and maintenance of the film processing plant at Rochester by Eastman Kodak.[1]

In 1956 Eastman Kodak also established an operation to covertly supply film for the U-2 programme, separated from its other commercial operations, producing the first 9.5ins rolls of 'Kodak Special Plus X Aerial Aerographic film.' At the other end of operations it was contracted by the CIA to undertake processing operations from Unit 7 of the Lincoln Plant, in Rochester, a former perfume factory, conveniently owned by the US Navy. Its early 25ft long Eltron processor had to have 150ft of film threaded through the machine before it could begin processing film at five feet per minute. It had to allow operators time to judge the level of film under or over-exposure, before processing it. The film was passed through a 'stop' solution to halt the development process. Using a safe dark light, the film was assessed by skilled technicians. If the exposure was correct it went through a secondary Eltron processor to fix the film, at the rate of 7.5ft a minute. If not sufficiently exposed it was developed further until ready, then fixed, washed and dried. This was a slow process, but it was progressively improved as better equipment was developed. The Lincoln plant was too small for necessary further expansion so operations soon moved to Kodak's Hawkeye plant (also in Rochester) as work for the CIA and NRO increased. It gained the codename 'Bridgehead.' As the film processing neared completion a USAF aircraft would be sent to Rochester Airport to pick up the consignment and take it to Andrews AFB for distribution. Over the many years of CIA U-2 operations Kodak employees, as part of a 'Technical Assistance' group also operated along deployed U-2s at locations including, Taiwan, Germany, Thailand, Turkey and the Philippines. The company also played a key role in assisting the NRO and USAF to develop their processing capabilities.

Air Force Special Projects Production Facility

Westover AFB, MA, became a major player early on. It was used as a transhipment point for exposed film being couriered to the US for processing and moving the finished material onto customers once processing was completed. From late 1955 until 1976, within Building P–1900 at Westover was the US Air Force Special Projects Production Facility (AFSPPF). It was created as an alternate facility to Eastman Kodak's and served as a backup location for the NROs photo-reconnaissance activities. It maintained a storage facility for processing, film developing equipment and materials.[2] Operated by a mix of 56 officers and civilians, plus around 280 enlisted personnel, most with specialist experience and the required high-level security clearances. Even the existence of the unit was officially denied.

The 23ft long Trenton processor was the key step in developing the unexposed film into useable imagery. (CSNR/Bridgehead Archive)

The workloads of EK and the AFSPPF varied constantly as processing priorities changed. Arrivals of large bulks of materials for processing at either location would see additional work diverted to the other. Complications could arise if a deployed operation generated large amounts of photographic material from several missions and they were shipped back to the US as bulk loads. Work was near constantly re-prioritised. Couriers from the unit were responsible for collecting and delivering unprocessed materials from across the world, required to accompany them at all times. In the early days, they were often moved by C-47s and C-54s, later Military Airlift Command C-130s and even aboard civil airlines.

AFSPPF was an industrial-scale operation involving highly skilled technicians, operating complex machines, using copious amounts of dangerous chemicals and highly flammable materials. They often worked in conjunction with personnel from Eastman Kodak. Like them, when the original exposed material arrived, it was unpacked in a completely dark environment and any necessary repairs and splices made to the film before it was processed. It was not unusual for film to become torn or scratched in some way whilst it passed through the U-2's cameras. From long missions the whole procedure could take two to three days, even working on a 24-hour basis. Once processed the film was chopped into manageable lengths and quality control checked. A duplicate set of

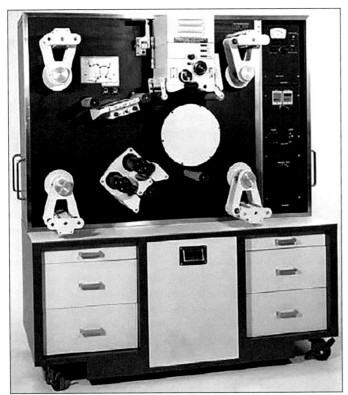

Machines like the Niagara III high-quality printer were designed and built by Bridgehead's engineers and photo scientists to produce the high-quality imagery needed by the Photo Interpreters. (CSNR/Bridgehead Archive)

Table 6: 1957 U-2 film reproduction scales[†]

Organisation	Original Negative	Prints	Duplicate positives	Duplicate Negatives
CIA: Main camera (A,B)	1	1	1	1
Tracker	1		1	
USAF: Main camera (A,B)			2	
Tracker			1	
USN: Main camera (A,B)			1	1
Tracker				

[†] Source: CIA-RDP92B01090R002600070017-5

master negatives would be produced, the precious original film sent to NPIC for storage. From the duplicate negatives, working positive prints were created on high-capacity printers after which they were packaged and sent onto the AFSPPF's customers. From Table 6 it is possible to imagine that the packages of material from the Eastman Kodak, or AFSPPF, would be substantial for long missions which had generated some 6,000ft of main camera material and 1,000ft from the tracker cameras and then reproduced in various forms up to nine times for different users.

Sending the finished materials on to customers posed problems of its own. Packages from the Shipping Division did not have addresses on, they were just colour coded. The couriers picked completed 'packages' up for delivery to the location they were given. They worked alone or in small teams as required, dependent on the assignment. This sometimes involved travelling, nearly always armed, on civilian airlines or via military air transports out of McGuire AFB. The courier operation, known as 'Miniball', in many ways resembled modern airfreight parcel pickup and distribution services with courier aircraft sometimes making multiple pick-up and drop-offs. It became so large it operated around the clock and had special secure communication links to collection and distribution locations. Individual couriers recount stories of being flown to military bases, taxiing to remote locations on airfields where they were met by a van and a security crew. Following the exchange of appropriate passwords, the couriers handed over their containers of classified material to its new custodians and then disappeared again.[3]

Whilst processing support of U-2 operations in Europe and the Middle East for Detachment B was served by the 497th RTS at Wiesbaden, Bridgehead and AFSPPF, Pacific based operations posed challenges of a different order. The huge distances involved, the scale of activities and their sometimes 'tactical' nature were sufficient to justify the existence of another semi-permanent processing facility. The 67th RTS became heavily involved in dealing with U-2 operations when missions began from Taiwan in 1962.[4]

HT Automat to NPIC

In preparation for U-2 operations and anticipating a vast increase in imagery, the Photographic Interpretation Division (PID), was created within the CIA. As momentum grew its main office was readied at the Steuart building, in a run-down part of Washington DC during spring 1956. It was very successful largely due to its founder and first head, Art Lundhal. His idea of the PID saw it become a 'national center' that he wanted to be

The down at heel frontage of the Steuart Building in a poor part of Washington DC would never have been mistaken as the location for working and analysing some of the United States' most secret intelligence. The man visible between the two cars is said to be legendary photo-interpreter Dino Brugioni. (NPIC)

as 'apolitical' as possible, set apart from the normal Washington bureaucratic infighting. It was better known to those in the field as 'HT Automat.'[5] It was to become the centre of excellence for analysis and interpretation serving the many federal intelligence agencies in Washington DC.

Lundhal required imagery from each U-2 mission be handled by mixed service and Agency teams. Having a keen awareness of Washington political life, he worked hard to ensure PID operated in as 'neutral' a manner as possible. He tried to ensure that the determination of intelligence priorities and target selection was handled outside PID, well aware these would soon become very charged issues amongst the armed services and intelligence agencies. Even before 'live' operations began PID was staffed by some 90 CIA photo interpreters and 60 support staff. The Army committed another 90 photo interpreters and staff, the US Navy 10-12 whilst the US Air Force provided just a few liaison officers, seemingly sulking that not all aerial reconnaissance had not been placed under its control. That stance was regretted as it largely marginalised USAF influence within HTA and soon reversed.

Initially HTA distributed copies of photographic materials to the US Army, Navy, Air Force, National Security Agency, State Department and National Reconnaissance Office (whose existence was also not even admitted). Within the CIA copies were shared within several sections: Deputy Director for Intelligence, Deputy Director for Plans, Office for Current Intelligence, Office for Research and Reports, Office of Scientific Intelligence and the AQUATONE project office. That distribution changed over time as many reorganisations occurred.

Within HTA/NPIC prints and enlargements of the negatives were made for interpreters and analysts to work on. So, as well as the PIs there were others, like researchers who would comb through other material, often open source, to try and reveal information or contextual data to support whatever problem was being worked on. The potential benefits of a multi-disciplinary team from the different military services and other agencies brought varied expertise to HTA then NPIC. Even with all this available knowledge, there were still conundrums created by the arrival of imagery that HTA/NPIC were unable to resolve, even after drafting in external expertise to help.

Temporary Processing Facilities

In addition to the main facilities, for short periods of operations temporary arrangements were sometimes activated. The Eisenhower Administration sought imagery of British and French operations in the Mediterranean during summer 1956. 'Det. B' became active in Middle East flights after becoming operational at Adana on 11 September 1956. To minimise processing delays, rather than transfer film directly to the US, an improvised facility was established at Adana to undertake initial work. Known as 'URPIC–1' it was subordinated to the 497th RTS at Wiesbaden (URPIC-W). Once the film was transferred onto Wiesbaden USAF personnel, supplemented by PID staff, completed theatre level analysis of the U-2 imagery before it was sent onto the US.

A similar arrangement operated in the Pacific theatre. From Yakota (URPIC–Y) personnel were sometimes temporarily deployed to Clark AFB, in the Philippines, to manage imagery collected by CIA U-2 missions mounted from Subic Bay over Indonesia in 1958 and some Det C missions from Astugi, When activated the small sub-unit was referred to as 'URPIC–2.' It processed the imagery and undertook the initial analysis before sending it to Yakota.

A processing facility was also established in Taiwan, where among other work, it processed tracker camera film, taking a copy before sending the original negatives on to the US. Work was done by ROC staff, with representatives from Eastman Kodak and the Agency. It is likely, though unconfirmed, that they undertook more sophisticated processing work and completed IPIRs for at least some missions.

Photo Interpretation

Convention ran that the unit completing the processing also prepared the Initial Photo Interpretation Report (IPIR), referred to as 'first phase' exploitation. This required the PIs to search through the imagery and identify objects that were the mission's main objective. From the U-2's tracker camera its exact route was plotted on a map. Then objects of interest on the imagery poured over by the PIs and identified and quantified. For perhaps a simple tactical mission, where the target was, say, a single port, that would often be a relatively simple task. But from U-2 missions where the results were measured in thousands of feet, particularly when it was over areas never imaged before, it could take a team of PIs some days to complete their examination. These IPIR messages could be many pages long, often sent in parts, passed to higher headquarters and other designated recipients. The IPIR could be revised if omissions or mistakes were identified, but there was only one IPIR. It meant that the message recipients had an idea of what items particularly interested them when processed film material became available. The aim was always to complete the IPIR as quickly and thoroughly as possible. The second phase exploitation was a more detailed look at the imagery, when time permitted, to detect any errors or subjects missed.

Beyond that was third phase reporting. This normally took the form of a much more detailed evaluation of imagery. It could involve examining several sets of imagery from the same site to detect changes and developments. Equally, it might compare, for example, several different SA-2 sites to compare layouts, types of radar, support equipment at each site to try and explain the similarities and differences.

Photo Interpretation is a skilled occupation. Well-trained PIs were strong on equipment identification skills, particularly from odd angles and slightly 'fuzzy' imagery. They were proficient at identifying potential subjects of interest, uses of industrial sites, civil and military infrastructure, town and city layouts, essentially the whole range of human activity that could be seen from above. That required not just good training but also accumulated knowledge and experience. Challenges arose when previously unseen equipment or unfamiliar installations layouts and structures were seen for the first time.

At increasing angles from the vertical the imagery became less valuable to the PIs, analysts and map makers. One way to increase its value, particularly for use in target materials and maps, would be to 'convert' imagery to the vertical plane. The process known as orthorectification is particularly important for map-making from imagery not taken directly overhead and has importance for imagery too. It can be complex and has been eased with digital imagery manipulation, but before digital imagery methods had to be developed to achieve the same goal.[6] The men at the 67th RTS devised one method to achieve this. The image being 'rectified' had to be re-photographed whilst it was fixed on an angled easel to correct for the angle it was originally taken at, back to the vertical. They used a vertically mounted camera above the easel, its surface was tilted at a specific angle, left to right, determined by what position the original image was taken by the U-2's B camera. This was 10 degrees for R1 and L1 camera positions, 20 degrees for R2 and L2 (see Chapter 4). The easel was also tilted at a specific angle from back to front, rather than used in a traditional horizontal table position. Photographed again this combination of easel angle and placing the image 'off square' on it, essentially rectified the original image into a vertical one. Members of the 67th RTS determined that the method provided a positional accuracy of around 150ft on maps.[7]

Mozhaysk: A Riddle Wrapped in a Mystery, Inside an Enigma

Early U-2 missions over the Iron Curtain were voyages of discovery. Some targets like airfields, or ports, were easily identifiable. Others were not. On just the second flight over the USSR from Wiesbaden on 5 July 1956, Carmine Vito flew to Moscow and up to Kalinin during Mission 2014. As he approached Moscow, on the leg from Smolensk, just before reaching Kubinka airfield, his A-2 camera array photographed some construction work. Just two images of the site soon attracted a great deal of time and huge effort across the US intelligence community over the next couple of years to determine its function.

Around the town of Mozhaysk, approximately 80 miles west-southwest of Moscow, there were a significant number of ammunition storage sites. One was of particular interest because of some unusual structures photographed. It was initially identified: 'simply as an unidentified housing and institutional area with one building hemispherical in shape.' However, within a couple of months, attention was turned towards it as a 'target of considerable interest' with no similar structures spotted elsewhere. 'By the latter part of August several informal PI-analyst conferences had been held concerning the Mozhaysk installation.' In September 1956 it was thought the site might be the beginnings of a nuclear reactor.

A later HT Automat history describes the facility well:

The installation was located in rural surroundings, about 75 miles west-southwest of Moscow. Within the site, which covered about three square miles, attention was centered on a large earth-covered dome 190 feet in diameter and 85 feet high, with a cap on top measuring 54 feet in diameter and 18 feet in thickness. A second structure, the mirror image of the first was situated one kilometre to the north. This second one was still under construction at the time of photography, revealing, among other internal details, a vertical shaft 24 feet in diameter under the position of the cap in the earth-covered dome. The operational part of the site contained many other buildings, some with massive walls up to 10 feet thick. Four major structures were buried or about to be buried to a depth of 20 feet or more. The entire site was surrounded by a double fence separated by a cleared strip 10 feet wide. Access was limited to one entrance provided with a guard post. All housing, which, it was estimated, would accommodate up to a few thousand persons, was within the security fence, but separated by another fence from the operational area. Some 10 miles of hard-surfaced roads with wide-angle turns connected the housing areas and facilities within the operational area. Many of the latter were individually fenced. Access from the outside was by a first-class road but there was no direct rail service. There was likewise no evidence of unusually large sources of water or electricity, or large-capacity facilities to dissipate heat from industrial processes.[8]

No positive determination was made of Mozhaysk's function, so a conference was held on 3 January 1957 that involved 49 experts from the armed forces, CIA, NSA and Atomic Energy Commission. Views ranged from it being a nuclear-powered rocket launch facility, conventional ICBM launch facility, nuclear

power plant, a test facility for nuclear components. However, in the absence of confirmatory intelligence, these were just speculations. Most focussed on nuclear-related activities. For the last two weeks of January 1957 the site engaged the full-time efforts of specialists in HT Automat's industrial, technical branches and others.

On 7 March 1957 the net was cast still wider, with outside experts, including representatives of the Lawrence Livermore Laboratory, Ramo-Wooldridge, Atomic Energy Commission, MIT and the California Institute of Technology all took part in another one-day conference. Former Nazi rocket pioneer Werner von Braun even participated. Not cleared into the AQUATONE, he was not allowed to be present for all of the conference or informed of the real source of the imagery. Shown a carefully degraded image he was told it had been surreptitiously taken by a 35mm camera from the window of an overflying aircraft. Again, the deliberations were inconclusive. Work continued and among the theories advanced contemplated Mozhaysk was to become an operational IRBM site, though that idea did not survive scrutiny. Attention was drawn by PIs to a site near Sebastopol in the Crimea where similar constructions were discovered. It was later identified as a cruise missile launch site.

The US intelligence community learned several lessons from trying to determine the use of Mozhaysk. First that photographic intelligence, vital as it was, required wider, all source, data in many situations. It emphasised the value of well-trained PIs, able to make informed initial judgements on what they were seeing. Recognition that PIs and analysts sometimes needed support from other disciplines such as engineers, those with knowledge of nuclear technology, missile and weapon design and so on, to help them better understand what they were looking at. The early imagery collection efforts also demonstrated the value of good graphic artists, able to distil key information from photographs into a form that could more easily be understood in presentations to non-intelligence trained senior military officers, civilians and officials.

There were calls for the site to be overflown again, but its proximity to Moscow made that most unlikely. It was not until the arrival of Corona satellites in 1960 that overhead coverage became possible again. Meanwhile, work on Mozhaysk took a back seat as a wealth of other imagery arrived for examination and analysis arrived and no obvious answer emerged about its real use. The function of the two domed structures has not been publicly revealed, though little doubt other intelligence exists and remains secret.

By 1970 the site was classified as one of several Soviet 'Sensitive Operation Complexes' (SOC) in an Agency Directorate of Science and Technology Report. Mozhaysk was assessed as being a nuclear storage site, though probably when they are broken down, with no missiles or missile handling facilities spotted at this or similar SOC sites.[9] Modern sources describe the facility today, named as Mozhaysk-10, as one of 12 'national-level storage facilities.' It is the closest to Moscow, most probably associated with Tver (Migalovo) Air Base. There the resident transport aircraft could move, most likely tactical weapons, between locations. Migalovo has its own nuclear storage facility (two miles to the west of the air base) which is possibly used for storage of materials moved to/from Mozhaysk, approximately 100 miles to the south.[10] In 2019 the Federation of American Scientists reported the upgrading of the nuclear storage facilities at both Mozhaysk-10 and Tver.[11]

MOZHAYSK

A small cottage industry studied the unusual structures at Mozhaysk for nearly 18 months based on just two images taken during Mission 2014, flown by Carmine Vito on 5 July 1956.

In what was an incredible piece of luck, these images revealed what became two identical mounds, described by Photo Interpreters as 'units.' The first was complete, the second under construction showing the underground parts of the structure that would soon be buried. The images should have been key to determining the Mozhaysk facility's function. They were not. Instead, they triggered a whole set of examinations by a wide range of experts that never reached clear conclusions at the time.

From Mission 2014's two images graphic artists produced drawings of key elements. The drawings reproduced here, were part of the HTA's first-ever Photographic Intelligence Report (HTA-R1-57). It is described as a copious volume full of images and detailed drawings, almost certainly of much better definition than these declassified samples. Unfortunately, the full report, with its accompanying drawings and photographs, remains classified. Even the images here give some indication of the additional materials PIs and analysts used to complete their work.

A graphic artist's view of the completed Unit 1, exactly one kilometre south of Unit 2. Now all that is visible is the mound and associated above-ground structures. These give little clue to its function. Imaging what soon became underground structures during their construction was considerable luck. (CIA)

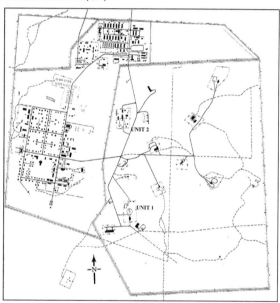

A map of the overall site with domestic support and housing sites. In the 1956 imagery both were within the fenced boundary to the Mozhaysk site, though separate from the operational area, showing the high security accorded to it. (CIA)

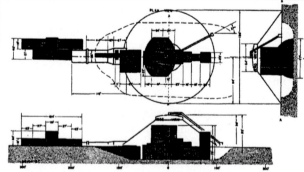

Two drawings of 'Unit 2', under construction at the time of the overflight, were used to show the extensive underground structures that would eventually be covered over. One produced in an oblique style view, with the other in a conventional plan form with estimated dimensions. (CIA)

Commercial satellite imagery taken in 2019 shows that security fencing to the domestic sites has disappeared and parts have been completely redeveloped. Research by Hans Kristensen and the FAS shows recent changes to the site and its further extension. But both the original 'Unit 1' and 'Unit 2' remain and the area around them cared for. (Kristensen/FAS)

Bison Central

In other situations, all source intelligence was vital for the construction of an accurate and reliable intelligence picture. Without it the imagery from U-2 missions alone often represented just isolated observations.

Mozhaysk was not Carmine Vito's only coup that July day, 1956. Examples of his almost vertical imagery taken over Moscow are contained in a January 1958 CIA PID report covering the Fili aircraft plant, near the city centre that built 'Bison' bombers.[12] Close by, on the edge of Moscow is Ramenskoye airfield, today known as Zhukovosky. It is a sprawling, still important, test facility for the Russian aerospace industry. The very first Myasishcev M-4 Bison had been spotted on the ground in 1953. However, it was not until 14 February 1955 that Fili was identified as the main production location for the new aircraft. Known as Airframe Plant Number 23, it was located in a large loop of the River Moskva, just 3.7nm west of the Kremlin. It was effectively surrounded by the river on three sides, with a runway less than 5,000ft long ending close to the river at each end. Bomber production plants were an early high priority intelligence target, a reason why it was specifically overflown by Mission 2014.

Whilst those few images from Vito's overflight were vital, without the additional intelligence collected from other sources on Fili over the next few years, it would have remained just an isolated observation. The 1958 PID report, parts of which remain redacted, gives a much broader picture of intelligence information collected on Fili from 1955–58. It is a combination of ground observations, likely from US Embassy staff who perhaps legitimately drove past the airfield on their daily commute to the office, as it was less than five miles from the US Embassy. Likely the airfield was deliberately targeted sometimes. On several separate occasions over three months from February 1955, single Bisons were observed on the ground, and taking-off on three more. At other times ground-level images show radar components sitting in the 'radar assembly area.'[13] The plant had been a wartime bomber production site, one of only three large bomber assembly plants in the entire USSR. New construction

was observed in 1954, with the erection of three large sheds close to the western end of the site and completed during 1956. Detailed overhead maps of the site are accompanied by estimates of building usage and a small number of images from that 5 July 1956 overflight.

The short length of the runway suggested that the new aircraft were only loaded with sufficient fuel to get them to nearby Ramenskoye for further flight testing. On 22 September 1955: 'a Bison was observed in transit on a barge moving downstream on the Moskva.' It was probably being moved to Ramenskoye, approximately 29 miles south-east of Fili, also along the course of the river Moskva. Later in the year air movements were seen again, as they were on the river too and at least once by the road along Sadovaya Street, a large ring road around part of central Moscow. From detailed descriptions of known aircraft movements, the Bisons subsequently sat on the Fili ramp for nearly three weeks each, as communications, functional, fuel, engine and other checks were believed to be completed.

The projected Bison numbers at that time were based on several mass sightings that have since grown into folklore. They illustrate the fragility of single-source intelligence assessments. Estimates were that by June 1957 cumulative Bison production

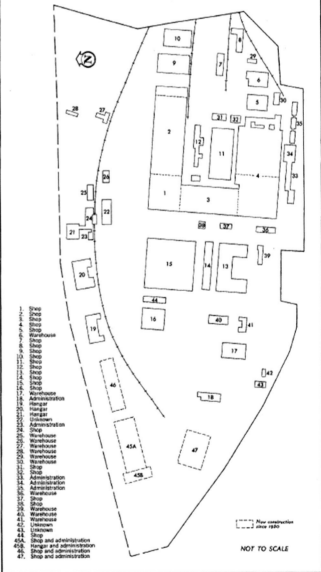

USSR: LAYOUT OF MOSCOW/FILI AIRFRAME PLANT NO. 23

1. Shop
2. Shop
3. Shop
4. Shop
5. Shop
6. Warehouse
7. Shop
8. Shop
9. Shop
10. Shop
11. Shop
12. Shop
13. Shop
14. Shop
15. Shop
16. Shop
17. Warehouse
18. Administration
19. Hangar
20. Hangar
21. Hangar
22. Unknown
23. Administration
24. Shop
25. Warehouse
26. Warehouse
27. Warehouse
28. Warehouse
29. Warehouse
30. Warehouse
31. Shop
32. Shop
33. Administration
34. Administration
35. Administration
36. Warehouse
37. Shop
38. Shop
39. Warehouse
40. Warehouse
41. Warehouse
42. Unknown
43. Unknown
44. Shop
45A. Shop and administration
45B. Hangar and administration
46. Shop and administration
47. Shop and administration

New construction since 1950

NOT TO SCALE

26221.2 9-57

Plan of the Fili Aircraft Plant drawn from imagery from Carmine Vito's flight over central Moscow. (CIA)

Carmine Vito imaged the Fili aircraft plant in central Moscow that produced M-4 Bison bombers in July 1956, part of a comprehensive collection effort. (CIA)

was 65 aircraft. In service, the Bison never lived up to its designer's promises, with poor range, heavy fuel consumption and frequent accidents. Estimates of total production up to 1963 vary between 93 to 116 airframes, although never more than 60 bombers appear to have been in service with Soviet Long-Range Aviation.[14] It was only through a combination of overhead (likely including post-1960 satellite data) and other observations that a reasonably comprehensive intelligence picture could be assembled on the Bison and the Fili Plant. It illustrates the importance for analysts of both repeat overflight observation and multi-source intelligence.

These are just two of many similar such examples of how CIA U-2 operations contributed to the assembly of high priority Cold War intelligence.

U-2 versus satellite

Comparison of U-2 imagery between missions, aircraft and early Corona satellites is a challenging task. The quality of imagery from the individual platforms varies enormously affected by a huge range of technical factors such as camera fit, how well the camera was initially set-up, the quality of the optics, how well the components function in extremes of temperature all contribute to final image quality. Then there are effects of the airframe carrying the camera. Vibrations affecting the airframe and levels of turbulence when taking photographs are additional factors.

Then there are a host of environmental factors. During U-2 missions the aircraft altitude varied. As altitudes change the level of detail recorded, the amount of ground coverage attained change too. Weather, especially cloud cover, angle of the sun, air temperatures and pollution levels all make a difference too. The angle of the shot and distance from the targets are all factors that can affect image quality and its resolution, the ability to distinguish different size objects. Virtually all these factors applied to the early satellite

imagery too. The early Corona satellites operated at 100-miles altitude and later ones closer at 75 miles above the Earth. They all combine to affect the quality of imagery and its ultimate value to interpreters. Sometimes the factors worked adversely to make what should be viable imagery unusable. Just occasionally, it brought remarkable enhancements such as for the 'High Wire' mission 8005 over the USSR on 6 December 1959.

Attempting to take all these factors into account it is useful to attempt a comparison between these sources to see what data can be distinguished by them. It is not a technical-scientific evaluation just an effort at simple comparison.[15] The two images are of the same area of central Moscow, a bend in the river Moskva near Moscow University. The two images were taken eight years apart. When the central feature of both images, the Central Lenin Stadium, is kept at a constant size the smallest just about discernible objects are individual vehicles, although no identification of type or size is possible.

Image A was taken directly overhead with image B originally photographed at an oblique angle. Image C, is the original oblique image from which B was 'rectified.' It can also look rather odd to the eye, a bit of an optical illusion. In places, it looks as if it is being viewed from directly overhead and elsewhere as if it has been photographed from quite a 'flat' angle. This is because of distortions in the image caused by another number of factors including the orientation of the sensor, topographical variations and curvature of the Earth. The imagery manipulation process to correct for these inaccuracies is orthorectification. It is that process that converts it to the overhead view.

Overhead image A was taken on 5 July 1956 by U-2 Mission 2014 using an A2 camera. Images B and C come from KH-4A Mission 1007 on 23 June 1964. It carried two J-1 panoramic cameras, 61cm focal length lenses with a stated ground resolution of 2.7m. With

Image A. Lenin Stadium in central Moscow, just a few weeks before it was officially opened. It was taken by U-2 Mission 2014 on 5 July 1956. (NARA via Lin Xu and Chris Pocock)

Image B. The same stadium in Moscow by KH-4A Corona Mission 1007 on 23 June 1964 after rectification. (CAST, https://corona.cast.uark.edu, accessed 8 March 2021)

Image C. The original KH-4A oblique image from Mission 1007 which was rectified to produce the overhead view. (CAST, https://corona.cast.uark.edu, accessed 8 March 2021)

final images of broadly comparable quality for photo interpretation purposes, we can get an indication of how long it took satellite imagery to qualitatively catch-up with that from the U-2, bearing in mind this is early A camera photography and eventually surpass it. In essence, the same systems in similar circumstances would achieve very different results on any individual day, given the large numbers of variables involved. Therefore, direct comparisons between the two are not always possible or even particularly useful.

The differences between the coverage of the individual frames from both system is simply remarkable. For U-2 Mission 2014 this A2 camera frame captured a ground area of 30 x 15kms. For the unmanned Corona J1 system, the single image capturing the stadium covered a swath of 275 x 18-23kms and is easy to see why their wide area coverage was so valuable. The huge advantage that the U-2 had was its flexibility. Planning and re-planning a U-2 mission was infinitely quicker and simpler than the schedules that had to be developed for undertaking KH-4 satellite missions.

Data Explosion

The sudden increase in available imagery generated first by U-2 missions, then satellite imagery, soon created a persistent challenge that has faced US intelligence agencies ever since. This was simply how to catalogue and record the material in a way that would make it easily accessible to those who needed it later. This may sound like a largely bureaucratic problem but it remains a very real one. First, the physical storage requirements mushroomed as the quantities of imagery grew. How could the data be stored in readily retrievable form for analysts and their 'customers'. From that, additional issues arose over secure physical custody, security clearances and who could see what. Storing and cataloguing this data was certainly an early case where computer technology was employed in an attempt to manage the material. Even with ever bigger storage solutions and sophisticated databases, the experiences of individuals and teams of photo interpreters and analysts were still vital for pulling together disparate, apparently unconnected, scraps of information and qualitative data. It was only with their knowledge and experience that comprehensive, detailed pictures of the many targets now imaged could be assembled.

Europe closes, Asia beckons

The shooting down of Gary Powers brought overflights of the Soviet Union to an abrupt end. It saw the closure of Detachment B including the evacuation of the British element and an end to CIA U-2 operations in Europe and the Middle East for some years.

The achievements of the U-2 programme up to May Day 1960 were considerable. It had produced approximately 25 miles of 70mm tracker film and the equivalent of a 220-mile strip of 9in intelligence film covering over 1.3 million square miles of territory (about 15 percent of its total area). In great secrecy it settled the successive 'bomber gap' and 'missile gap' arguments that had raged at near hysterical levels at times in the US Congress, accompanied by calls for ever increased defence spending to remedy perceived American weakness. The U-2 had successfully charted many elements of the Soviet nuclear programme from research establishments, test locations, depots, operational stores and bases. It had established key research and test locations for the Soviet chemical warfare programme. Beyond that it amassed a vast hoard of air, land and naval Order of Battle intelligence. It had witnessed at very close quarters the development, deployment and refinement of Soviet air defences, particularly as much of that effort was directed against the U-2 itself. Had the U-2 story finished there, it would still have been a remarkable achievement in a very short space of time. However, the U-2 was still too valuable an asset, even with its new-found vulnerability, to be dispensed with. It simply adapted to changed circumstances.[16]

The resources released by withdrawal from Europe and closure of Detachment B were used to establish a mobile capability, deployable worldwide based at Edwards AFB in California with the formation of Detachment G. It soon engaged in regular overseas operations and exercises up to the CIA's divestment of its U-2s in 1974.

In Asia operations had only just begun. Detachment C at Astugi AB in Japan undertook some initial overflights of the Soviet Far East. Fears of war between Communist and Nationalist Chinese across the Taiwan Straits, in 1958, prompted a short series of overflights to calm tensions. Deployed operations were mounted from Cubi Point in the Philippines to cover parts of Indonesia. Negotiations with the Taiwanese had begun, over a stationing U-2s there. These led to the establishment of Detachment H, based at Taoyuan, a joint US-Taiwanese operation, which commenced overflights in January 1962. Between then and 1974 missions across Asia formed the greater part of CIA U-2 activities. These led to regular staging operations based in Thailand, with others mounted from India and South Korea. From these bases, missions overflew all of the vast Peoples Republic of China, Tibet, North Korea, South Vietnam, North Vietnam, Laos, Cambodia and parts of French Polynesia, the latter from a US Navy aircraft carrier. It is these missions and the later return to Europe and Middle East that will be detailed in Volume 2.

Table 7: CIA and SAC U-2 Production

U-2A production	CIA	SAC	Total
Original	20	30	
USAF 1958 extra purchase		5	55

Table 8: Annual U-2 attrition by Article No.[†]

Year and Model	Date	Pilot Name (indicates fatal loss)	Airframes left at year end (based on total purchase of 55 U-2A although final deliveries not completed until March 1959).
1956			
345A	15 May		
354A	31 August	Frank Grace	
346A	17 September	Howard Carey	
357A	19 December		51
1957			
341A	4 April	Bob Sieker	
366A	28 June	Lieutenant Leo Smith	
369A	28 June	Lieutenant Ford Lowcock	
361A	26 September		
371A	22 November	Captain Benny Lacombe	
			46
1958			
380A	8 July	Squadron Leader Chris Walker, RAF	
365A	9 July	Captain Al Chapin Jr	
364A	6 August	Lieutenant Paul Haughland	
377A	11 September	Captain Pat Hunerwadel	
			42
1959			
	(no losses)		
			42
1960			
360C	1 May		
387A	14 July		
			40
[†]Sources: CIA CREST and Pocock, *50 years of the U-2*, pp.406–409.			

BIBLIOGRAPHY

Aldrich, R, *The Hidden Hand: Britain, America and Cold War Secret Intelligence* (London: John Murray, 2001)

Beschloss, M, *Mayday: Eisenhower, Khrushchev and the U-2 Affair* (London: Faber & Faber, 1986)

Bissell Jr, R, 'Origins of the U-2', *Air Power History*, Vol 36, No 4 (Winter 1989), pp.15–24.

Brugioni, D, *Eyes in the Sky: Eisenhower, the CIA and Cold War Aerial Espionage* (Anapolis: Naval Institute Press, 2010)

CIA, CREST: '*Utility Flight Handbook*,' March 1959, https://www.cia.gov/library/readingroom/docs/ DOC_0005729692.pdf

CIA, Directorate of Science & Technology, *History of the Office of Special Activities from Inception to 1969.*

Crampton, J, 'RB-45 Operations', Proceedings of the RAFHS Seminar on Cold War Intelligence Gathering, *RAF Historical Society Journal*, No. 23, (2001), pp.97–100.

Dabrowski, K, *Hunt for the U-2* (Warwick: Helion, 2020)

DTIC, *High Altitude Sampling Programme* (Washington DC, DASA,1961) https://apps.dtic.mil/dtic/tr/fulltext/u2/267616.pdf

Ford, K, *Swift and Sure: 80 Years of No 51 Squadron RAF* (Preston: Compaid Graphics, 1997)

Haight, D, 'Ike and His Spies in the Sky', *Prologue*, 41/4 (winter 2009), pp.14-27.

Hammer, E and Ur, J, 'Near Eastern Landscapes and Declassified U2 Aerial Imagery', *Advances in Archaeological Practice*, (2019), pp.1-20. DOI:10.1017/aap.2018.38.

Hersh, S M, *The Samson Option: Israel's Nuclear Arsenal and American Foreign Policy* (London: Random House, 1991)

Jackson, R, *High Cold War* (Yeovil: Patrick Stevens Ltd, 1998)

MIT, *Problems of Air Force Intelligence and Reconnaissance, 'Beacon Hill Report'*, 15 June 1952. https://www.governmentattic. org/12docs/USAF-BeaconHillReport 1952.pdf.

Novak, K, 'Rectification of Digital Imagery', *Photogrammetric Engineering & Remote Sensing*, Vol. 58, No. 3, March 1992, pp.339–344.

NRO-CSNR, *BRIDGEHEAD: Eastman Kodak Company's Covert Photo-reconnaissance Film Processing Programme* (Chatilly,VA: NRO-CSNR, 2014)

Pedlow G, and Welzenbach, D, *The CIA and Overhead Reconnaissance: The U-2 and Oxcart Programmes 1954-1974* (New York: First Skyhorse Publishing, 2016) pp.34-35.

Pocock, C, *50 years of the U-2: The complete illustrated history of the "Dragon Lady"* (Atglen PA: Schiffer Military History, 2005)

Powers, F G, and Gentry, C, *Operation Overflight: A Memoir of the U-2 Incident* (Washington DC: Brassey's, 2004)

Reade, D, 'U-2 Spy Planes: What You Didn't Know About Them,' *Air Power History*, Vol.58, No. 3, (Fall 2011), pp.6.-15.

Rich, B, Janos, L, *Skunk Works: A Personal Memoir of My Years at Lockheed* (London: Sphere, 1995)

Richelson, J, *American Espionage and The Soviet Target* (New York: William Morrow and Company, 1987)

Riste, O, *Norwegian Intelligence Service 1945-1970* (Abingdon: Routledge, 2013)

Spanberger, L, *Our Mission Revealed* (Bloomington, IN: Xlibris Publishing, 2014)

Tamnes, R, *The US and the Cold War in the High North* (Aldershot: Dartmouth Publishing, 1991)

Taubman, P, *Secret Empire: Eisenhower, the CIA and the Hidden Story of America's Space Espionage* (New York: Simon and Schuster, 2003)

USAF, *AF(C)-1-1,U-2C and U-2F Flight Manual*, https://info. publicintelligence.net/USAF-U2.pdf

Welzenbach, D and Galyean, N, 'Those Daring Young Men and Their Ultra-High-Flying Machines', *Studies in Intelligence*, Vol. 31, No. 3, (1987), pp.103-115.

Wright, K, *The Collectors: US and British Cold War Aerial Intelligence Gathering* (Warwick: Helion, 2019)

Wright, K, 'Stratospheric Cold War Warriors: Alconbury's TR-1As', *Aviation News*, Vol. 82, No. 3, (March 2020), pp.24-28.

Zabetakis, S, J Peterson, 'The Diyarkabir Radar', *Studies in Intelligence*, Vol. 8, No. 3, pp.41-47, (1964).

Zaloga, S, *The Kremlin's Nuclear Sword* (London: Smithsonian Press, 2002)

Online Archive Sources

Central Intelligence Agency

CIA Records Search Tool (CREST): https://www.cia.gov/library/ readingroom/

Eisenhower Presidential Library

Eisenhower Presidential Archive: https://www.eisenhower. archives.gov/

Foreign Relations of the United States (FRUS)

State Department, Office of the Historian: https://history.state.gov/

UK National Archive

The UK National Archive: http://www.nationalarchives.gov.uk/

US National Archive

https://www.archives.gov/

NOTES

Chapter 1

1. Crampton, 'RB-45 Operations,' p.130, 'Proceedings of the RAFHS Seminar on Cold War Intelligence Gathering,' *RAF Historical Society* Journal, No.23, 2001, pp.98-99.
2. MIT, *Problems of Air Force Intelligence and Reconnaissance*, 'Beacon Hill Report', 15 June 1952.
3. Gregory Pedlow and Donald Welzenbach, *The CIA and Overhead Reconnaissance: The U-2 and Oxcart Programmes 1954-1974*, (New York: First Skyhorse Publishing, 2016), pp.34-35.
4. Pedlow, *CIA Overhead*, p.39.
5. CIA-RDP33-02415A000100070069-7.
6. The project AQUATONE codename, used from December 1954, became CHALICE in April 1958 and then IDEALIST/TACKLE from May 1960.
7. Pedlow, *CIA Overhead*, pp.73-78.
8. USAF. *AF(C)-1-1, U-2C and U-2F Flight Manual*, https://info.publicintelligence.net/USAF-U2.pdf, p.222 (accessed 28 October 2020).
9. Pedlow, *CIA Overhead*, pp.58-59.
10. NRO-CSNR, (2014), *BRIDGEHEAD: Eastman Kodak Company's Covert Photo-reconnaissance Film Processing Programme*, (NRO-CSNR, Chatilly:VA), p.14.
11. Pedlow, *CIA Overhead*, pp.56-62.
12. CIA, Directorate of Science & Technology, *History of the Office of Special Activities from Inception to 1969*, p.411.
13. CIA-RDP89B00980R000400090011-0, Pedlow, *CIA Overhead*, pp.60-61. Taubman, P, *Secret Empire: Eisenhower, the CIA and the Hidden Story of America's Space Espionage*, (New York: Simon and Schuster, 2003), p.153.
14. In this instance the word 'focussed' should be interpreted to mean such a 'narrow field of view.' James Cunningham interview, CIA-RDP90B00170R000200240001- 6.pdf p.4.
15. CIA-RDP62b00844r000200090101-2.
16. CIA-RDP63-00313A0006000010002-3.
17. CIA-RDP67B00511R0001000010034-3.pdf.
18. CIA-RDP61-00763A000200030075-8.
19. Interview James A Cunningham, 4 October 1983, CIA-RDP90B00170R000200240001-6.
20. CIA, *History of the OSA*, p.415.
21. CIA, *History of the OSA*, pp.514-15, 522-24.
22. CIA, *History of the OSA*, pp.1729-1730.
23. CIA, *History of the OSA*, pp.1726-1727.
24. See Chapter 2.
25. CIA, *History of the OSA*, pp.468-489.
26. CIA, *History of the OSA*, pp.469-470.
27. CIA-RDP89B00487R000400720023-8.
28. See Chapter 4 for a more detailed description of these operations.
29. CIA, *History of the OSA*, pp.471-472.
30. CIA, *History of the OSA*, pp.472-476.
31. CIA, '*Utility Flight Handbook*,' March 1959, pp.5.13 to 5.16.
32. Reade, D, 'U-2 Spy Planes: What You Didn't Know About Them,' *Air Power History*, Vol.58, No.3, (Fall 2011), pp.6-15.
33. CIA, CREST: '*Utility Flight Handbook*,' p.4-40.
34. DTIC, *High Altitude Sampling Programme*, (Washington DC, DASA,1961) https://apps.dtic.mil/dtic/tr/fulltext/u2/267616.pdf, p.71, pp.230-232.
35. CIA, '*Utility Flight Handbook*,' pp.4-40 to 4-47.
36. https://apps.dtic.mil/dtic/tr/fulltext/u2/267616.pdf p.109. This reference contains a great deal of detail on the organisation and conduct of the HASP programme.
37. CIA-RDP61S00750A000200070043-4
38. CIA-RDP81B00879R000100010028-3
39. K. Wright, 'Stratospheric Cold War Warriors: Alconbury's TR-1As,' *Aviation News*, Vol.82, No.3, (March 2020), pp.24-28.
40. http://www.analogmuseum.org/library/asn6.pdf (accessed 29 October 2020). CIA, '*Utility Flight Handbook*,' p.5-16.
41. Pocock, C, *50 years of the U-2: The complete illustrated history of the "Dragon Lady*,' (Atglen PA: Schiffer Military History, 2005). Pocock, p.90.
42. It was later converted to a U-2F.
43. CIA, '*Utility Flight Handbook*,' p.4-54.
44. CIA, '*Utility Flight Handbook*,' p.5-13.
45. CIA-RDP63-00313A000600030033-7.
46. CIA-RDP81B00878R001300070087-1.
47. Reade, '*U-2 Spy Planes*,' pp.7-15.

Chapter 2

1. CIA, *History of the OSA*, pp.817-818.
2. CIA, *History of the OSA*, p.788.
3. Pedlow, *CIA Overhead*, p.107.
4. CIA-RDP33-02415A000100100046-8.
5. CIA-RDP62B00844R000200010162-3.
6. CIA-RDP04T00184R000400010001-1.
7. CIA-RDP89B00709R000500970011-6.
8. https://www.cia.gov/library/readingroom/docs/CIA-RDP80T00246A050400610001-4.pdf, https://www.cia.gov/library/readingroom/docs/CIA-RDP80T00246A054100090001-1.pdf, CIA-RDP04T00184R000400010001-1, pp.80-83.
9. CIA-RDP89B00709R000500970007-1.
10. CIA-RDP62B00844R000200200033-5. pdf.Taubman, *Secret Empire*, p.177.
11. Taubman, *Secret Empire*, p.184.
12. Michael Beschloss, *Mayday: Eisenhower, Khrushchev and the U-2 Affair* (London: Faber & Faber, 1986), p.133.
13. CIA-RDP79S01057A000200040017-6.
14. FRUS, 1950-55, The Intelligence Community, 1950-55: Note from executive Secretary of the NSC, 15 March 1954.
15. *President Dwight Eisenhower Aerial Intelligence Development Papers*, pp.15-16.http://www.paperlessarchives.com/FreeTitles/EisenhowerAerialIntelligence.pdf (accessed 22 September 2020).
16. David Haight, 'Ike and His Spies in the Sky,' *Prologue*, 41/4 (winter 2009) pp.14-27.
17. Beschloss, *Mayday*, p.132.
18. J Richelson, *American Espionage and The Soviet Target* (New York: William Morrow and Company, 1987), pp.145-146.
19. CIA-RDP04T00184R000400010001-1 p.23.
20. CIA, *History of the OSA*, pp.809-810, Pedlow, *CIA Overhead*, p.123.
21. CIA, *History of the OSA*, p.810.
22. CIA, *History of the OSA*, p.860.
23. Pedlow, *CIA Overhead*, pp.122-129. CIA, *History OSA*, pp.858-859, 863.
24. Robert Jackson, *High Cold War* (Yeovil: Patrick Stevens Ltd, 1998), p.110.

25. CIA-RDP89B00551R000600300001-1, CIA-RDP89B00551R000600300004-8, CIA-RDP89B00551R000600300018-3.
26. Pedlow, *CIA Overhead*, pp.134-135.CIA-RDP81B00878R000200050098-3, CIA-RDP89B00551R000600320044-2.
27. CIA, *History of the OSA*, pp.60, 1764.
28. CIA, *History of the OSA*, p.468.
29. CIA-RDP62B00844R000200100057-0.
30. D. Welzenbach and N Galyean, 'Those Daring Young Men and Their Ultra-High-Flying Machines,' *Studies in Intelligence*, Vol.31, No.3, (1987), pp.104-105. See Chapter 5 for more details.
31. CIA-RDP81B00878R001400050033-1.
32. CIA, *History of the OSA*, p.877.
33. CIA-RDP81B00880R000100270017-6.
34. CIA-RDP92B01090R002600260016-5.
35. CIA-RDP89B00709R000501060009-8, CIA-RDP89B00709R000501050003-5, CIA-RDP89B00709R000501060004-3, CIA-RDP61S00750A000500030004-8, CIA-RDP78T05439A000200220045-0. See also Chapter 6 for more detailed examination.
36. CIA-RDP81B00878R000800130030-2, CIA-RDP65-00523R000100180048-1.
37. CIA-RDP33-02415A000500320008-2.
38. CIA-RDP89B00487R000300470001-1.
39. Ben Rich, and Leo Janos, *Skunk Works: A Personal Memoir of My Years at Lockheed* (London: Sphere, 1995), p.165.
40. CIA-RDP61S00750A000200080024-4, CIA-RDP78T04753A000700010007-9, CIA-RDP89B00551R000600370026-7.
41. Rich, *Skunk Works*, p.165.
42. CIA-RDP33-02415A000500320067-7.
43. CIA-RDP04T00184R000400010001-1 pp.160-161.
44. CIA-RDP84B00459R000100090001-8.pdf, pp.36-37.
45. CIA-RDP89B00551R000600380001-3, pp.14-15, CIA-RDP04T00184R000400060001-6 pp.195-210.
46. https://www.bbc.com/future/article/20170926-the-deadly-germ-warfare-island-abandoned-by-the-soviets (accessed 3 July 2020).
47. Rich, *Skunk Works*, p.166.
48. J. Richelson, 'Spying on the Bomb,' (WW Norton: NY 2007), pp.117-119, Ben Rich, *Skunk Works*, pp.166-169.
49. https://www.cia.gov/library/center-for-the-study-of-intelligence/kent-csi/vol12no4/html/v12i4a01p_0001.htm.
50. CIA-RDP78T05693A000300030026-9.
51. CIA-RDP62B00844R000200070053-8.
52. CIA-RDP78T05693A000300040003-3.
53. Beschloss, *Mayday*, p.150.
54. CIA-RDP89B00487R000300470001-1.
55. CIA-RDP63-00313A000600010002-3.
56. CIA-RDP62B00844R000200240012-4.
57. Beschloss, *Mayday*, p.5.

Chapter 3

1. These included: TNA, AIR 40/2750, 2751, 2752 High Wire; AIR 40/2753 'Knife Edge;' AIR 40/2755 'Square Deal.'
2. Aldrich, R, *The Hidden Hand: Britain, America and Cold War Secret Intelligence*, (London: John Murray, 2001), p.529.
3. Brugioni, D, *Eyes in the Sky: Eisenhower, the CIA and Cold War Aerial Espionage*, (Annapolis: Naval Institute Press, 2010), pp.170-171.
4. CIA, *History of the OSA*, pp.906, 912, 985.
5. Paul Lashmar interview with Squadron Leader Robertson. https://www.youtube.com/watch?reload=9&v=h64a3d1yES4 (accessed 2 November 2020).
6. CIA, *History of the OSA*, p.910.
7. CIA, *History of the OSA*, p.916–917.
8. CIA, *History of the OSA*, p.911.
9. CIA, *History of the OSA*, p.953.
10. CIA, *History of the OSA*, p.917.
11. CIA, *History of the OSA*, pp.985-986.
12. TNA, AIR 40/2752, Proposed OLDSTER Mission - Cover Story, Doc 10, p.2.
13. CIA, *History of the OSA*, p.914.
14. CIA, *History of the OSA*, p.944.
15. Keith Ford, *Swift and Sure: Eight Years of No 51 Squadron RAF* (Preston: Compaid Graphics, 1997), p.261.
16. CIA, *History of the OSA*, p.961.
17. Personal conversations military Air Traffic Controller involved.
18. TNA, AIR 40/2744, Doc 34, 19 December 1958.
19. CIA, *History of the OSA*, p.870. C-130s replaced the early use of C-124s. For a more detailed description see Chapter 5.
20. CIA-RDP63-00313A000600030040-9.
21. CIA-RDP33-02415A000100190004-5.
22. CIA, *History of the OSA*, p.880.
23. CIA-RDP89B00569R000300110001-5.
24. CIA-RDP89B00569R000300110001-5, CIA-RDP63-00313A000600030027-4.
25. CIA-RDP89B00569R000400080067-0.

Chapter 4

1. Robbie Robertson interview Paul Lashmar.
2. TNA, AIR 40/2744, DDOPS(D)/TS50, Huddleston to SoS 5 January 1959.
3. E Hammer and J Ur, (2019), 'Near Eastern Landscapes and Declassified U2 Aerial Imagery,' *Advances in Archaeological Practice*, 2019, pp.1-20. DOI:10.1017/aap.2018.38
4. TNA, AIR 40/2744, D.D.Ops.(D)/TS.5009 SoS from VCAS 5 January 1959. S362 PM from SoS, January 1959. S578 PM 3 February 1959.
5. CIA-RDP33-02415A000300290091-6.
6. CIA-RDP89B00551R000400130013-9.
7. CIA-RDP89B00551R000400130019-3.
8. Pedlow, *CIA Overhead*, pp.156-157.
9. CIA, *History of the OSA*, p.860.
10. More details of the processing effort are in Chapter 9.
11. Rich, *Skunk Works*, p.159.
12. CIA, *Utility Flight Handbook*, 4-18 to 4-29.
13. TNA, AIR 40/2744, Bingham-Hall to PUSD 9, January 1959.
14. Brugioni, *Eyes in the Sky*, p.271.
15. CIA-RDP61S00750A000200110038-5.
16. CIA-RDP33-02416A000300020001-6. p.5, CIA-RDP78T05439A000100080002-1.
17. Brugioni, *Eyes in the Sky*, pp.271-273. Seymour Hersh, *The Samson Option: Israel's Nuclear Arsenal and American Foreign Policy* (London: Random House, 1991), pp 52-58.
18. Mission B1426 CIA-RDP78T05447A000200010027-4, Mission B8604 CIA-RDP78T05693A000200020036-0.
19. Examples: KWCORK is Adana, KWCROWN-19 is Wg Cdr Bingham-Hall, KWHIBAL U-2 with J-75 engine.
20. TNA, AIR 40/2744, VCAS from AVM Grandy, 1 December 1958.

21. https://dataverse.harvard.edu/file.xhtml?persistentId=doi:10.7910/DVN/VD74QX/W21LFO&version=1.0
22. CIA-RDP67B00511R000100250001-3.
23. S Zabetakis, J Peterson, (1964), 'The Diyarkabir Radar,' *Studies in Intelligence*, Vol 8, Fall, pp.41–47.
24. CIA-RDP78B05700A000400200029-5.
25. Https://www.youtube.com/watch?v=h64a3d1yES4.
26. Missions 1562 and 1563 have been forgotten from U-2 flight history totals because they were incorrectly numbered. As the CIA itself says these: 'should have been flown within the 4000 series.' They were certainly flown as there are routes and mission reports for each.
27. CIA-RDP89B00551R000400300003-1.
28. CIA-RDP67B00511R000100300009-9.
29. CIA-RDP89B00551R000400290014-1.

Chapter 5

1. O. Riste, *Norwegian Intelligence Service 1945–1970* (Abingdon: Routledge, 2013), p.273.
2. CIA, *History of the OSA*, pp.872, 875–876, 881–882.
3. CIA-RDP61S00750A000200060164-1.
4. CIA, *History of the OSA*, p.1764.
5. Welzenbach, 'Daring Young Men,' pp.106–113.
6. Riste, *Norwegian Intelligence*, p.66.
7. Welzenbach and Galyean, 'Daring Young Men,' p.113.
8. Brugioni, *Eyes in the Sky*, pp.242–243. CIA, *History of the OSA*, p.1764.
9. Pedlow, *CIA Overhead*, Declassified 19 September 2016, p.141. https://www.archives.gov/files/declassification/iscap/pdf/2014-004-doc01.pdf, (accessed 18 September 2018).
10. R Tamnes, *The US and the Cold War in the High North* (Aldershot: Dartmouth Publishing, 1991), p,175.
11. Riste, *Norwegian Intelligence*, pp.67–68.
12. CIA, *History of the OSA*, pp.814–815.
13. Brugioni, *Eyes in the Sky*, p.243. Details of HT Automat's early interaction with the Norwegians are still redacted in its own history CIA-RDP04T00184R000400030001-9 pp.446–449.
14. CIA, *History of the OSA*, pp.872–873.
15. In a few CIA documents there are passing references to this Bodø deployment being to 'Det D.' If this was some informal reference or a semi-official one is unclear.
16. Riste, *Norwegian Intelligence*, p.67.
17. Tamnes, *Cold War in the High North*, pp.132–133, 176.
18. CIA, *History of the OSA*, pp.874–875.
19. Tamnes, *Cold War in the High North*, p.132.
20. F G Powers, and C Gentry, *Operation Overflight: A Memoir of the U-2 Incident* (Washington DC: Brasseys, 2004), pp.48–49.
21. Pocock, *50 years of the U-2*, p.77.
22. CIA-RDP90B00170R000200170020-3, CIA-RDP33-02415A000300090125-0.
23. https://www.cia.gov/library/readingroom/docs/CENTRAL%20INTELLIGENCE%20BULL%5B15777314%5D.pdf
24. Riste, *Norwegian Intelligence*, pp.199–200.
25. CIA-RDP89B00569R000400020008-1.
26. Riste, *Norwegian Intelligence*, p.67.
27. CIA-RDP89B00569R000400020028-9.
28. CIA-RDP89B00569R000400020008-1.
29. CIA-RDP89B00551R000800010015-6, Chris Pocock, *50 years of the U-2*, p.77.
30. CIA-RDP89B00551R000800010011-0.
31. CIA-RDP61S00750A000600110086-8.
32. CIA-RDP63-00313A000600020079-8.
33. Richard Bissell Jr, Origins of the U-2, *Air Power History*, Vol 36, No 4 (Winter 1989), pp.15–24.
34. Tamnes, *Cold War in the High North*, p.177.
35. CIA, *History of the OSA*, pp.875, 1769.
36. CIA, *History of the OSA*, p.876.
37. Riste, *Norwegian Intelligence*, p.67.
38. CIA-RDP89B00551R000800120001-9, CIA-RDP78B05700A000100020003-2.
39. CIA-RDP78T05693A000300030034-0.
40. Rich, *Skunk Works*, pp.161–162.
41. CIA-RDP89B00569R000400070001-3.
42. Brugioni, *Eyes in the Sky*, pp.336–337.
43. TNA, Air 40/2744, SoS from VCAS, Project OLDSTER, November 1958.
44. TNA, AIR 40/2750, Bufton from Bissell, Doc 7C, November 1959 and Washington to Air Ministry (ACAS (I)), Ref.4164 10 November 1959.
45. TNA AIR 40/2750, To PM, Operation 'Oldster', 27 November 1959.
46. CIA-RDP89B00569R000400050002-4.
47. CIA RDP89B00569R000400050002-4.
48. TNA, AIR 40/2751, Appendix F, DD OPS (D)/TS.5026, 23rd December, 1959.
49. CIA RDP89B00569R000400050002-4.
50. Youtube: https://www.youtube.com/watch?v=h64a3d1yES4.
51. CIA RDP89B00569R000400050002-4.
52. CIA, *History of the OSA*, p.939.
53. TNA, AIR 40/2755, Doc 37, 7 January 1960. Joint Mission Coverage B8009, 5 February 1960, (CIA-RDP90B00224R000300380005-6).
54. CIA-RDP90B00224R000300380005-6.
55. TNA, AIR 40/2755, Doc 28, 6 January 1960.
56. http://www.military-today.com/bases/arzamas_16.htm (accessed 5 November 2020).
57. AIR 40/2755 TNA, Doc 30, 27 January 1960.
58. TNA, AIR 40/2755, to Sir P Dean from RWJ Hooper, January 22, 1960.
59. TNA, AIR 40/2755, From Steakley to Oldster, Oldster Square Deal, Doc 22.
60. TNA, AIR 40/2755, Oldster, 29 January 1960, Doc 38.
61. TNA, AIR 40/2755.
62. TNA, AIR 40/2755, Cable dated 1905Z/06 Doc 54. Until that time the Mission was 8011, one of the British sequence.
63. CIA-RDP89B00569R000400060047-4.
64. TNA AIR 40/2755 Oldster cable, April 12/13, 1960, Doc 122 and 123.
65. K. Dabrowski, *Hunt for the U-2* (Warwick: Helion, 2020), p.21.
66. Pocock, *50 years of the U-2*, pp.94–96.
67. CIA, *History of the OSA*, p.887.
68. CIA-RDP84B00459R000100010001-6.pdf, pp.40–41. This description matches very well that later published in his own account in F G Powers, and C Gentry, *Operation Overflight: A Memoir of the U-2 Incident* (Washington DC: Brasseys, 2004), pp.61–62.
69. CIA-RDP80B01676R002200080007-5.pdf.
70. CIA-RDP80B01676R002200040003-3.pdf.
71. CIA-RDP84B00459R000100090001-8.pdf, pp.1–2.
72. CIA-RDP84B00459R000100090001-8.pdf, p.6.
73. CIA-RDP80B01676R002200040003-3.pdf, CIA-RDP80B01676R002200080007-5.pdf.
74. Conversation Col Don Emmons, 26 October 2020.

Chapter 6

1. CIA, *History of the OSA*, pp.1716-1717.
2. CIA-RDP79B01709A001300010001-7, CIA-RDP76B00734R000100220002-5.
3. L Spanberger, *Our Mission Revealed*, (Bloomington, Indiana: Xlibris Publishing, 2014).
4. Details of 67th RTS' activities is covered in Volume 2 of this title.
5. HT Automat was renamed Photo Interpretation Center in August 1958 and National Photographic Intelligence Center on 25 January 1961.
6. For a more detailed exploration see: K Novak, 'Rectification of Digital Imagery,' *Photogrammetric Engineering & Remote Sensing*, Vol.58, No.3, March1992, pp.339-344.
7. Stanley, *Asia From Above*, pp.182, 214.
8. https://archive.org/details/NationalPhotographicInterpretationCenterTheYearsOfProject HTAUTOMAT, p.69, pp.94–106. (accessed 11 November 2020).
9. https://www.archives.gov/files/declassification/iscap/pdf/2012-033-doc1.pdf, p.15. (accessed 11 November 2020).
10. https://unidir.org/files/publications/pdfs/lock-them-up-zero-deployed-non-strategic-nuclear-weapons-in-europe-en-675.pdf. (accessed 11 November 2020).
11. https://fas.org/blogs/security/2019/07/russia-upgrades-western-nuclear-weapons-storage-sites/ (accessed 11 November 2020).
12. https://www.cia.gov/library/readingroom/document/0000491496. (accessed 11 November 2020)
13. CIA-RDP78B04560A001200010029-4.
14. S, Zaloga, *The Kremlin's Nuclear Sword* (London: Smithsonian Press, 2002), p.26.
15. I have controlled the reproduction qualities as far as possible to make the images comparable. The 2014 image was brightened and the satellite imaged darkened to adjust for original respective under and overexposure to improve them for publication.
16. CIA, *History of the OSA*, pp.1737-1747.

ABOUT THE AUTHOR

Having taught Cold War history, international security and politics at the University of Essex, Kevin Wright is a regular contributor to several UK aviation magazines. Publications have included books on Cold War aerial intelligence, articles on contemporary topics such as Bundeswehr Special Forces, Finnish Air Force F-18 operations and many others. He holds a PhD in international relations and is an experienced academic teacher and researcher. His lifelong interest in military aviation coupled with aerial photographic work makes him well qualified to examine and evaluate Cold War aerial intelligence collection.

Kevin is also the author of *The Collectors: US and British Cold War Aerial Intelligence Gathering*, published by Helion in 2019.